The Everest
Politics Show

*Sorrow and strife on the
world's highest mountain*

MARK HORRELL

Published by Mountain Footsteps Press

Copyright © 2016 Mark Horrell
www.markhorrell.com
All rights reserved

First published as an ebook 2016
Paperback edition published 2017

ISBN (paperback): 978-0-9934130-6-3
ISBN (ebook): 978-0-9934130-5-6

"I would gladly at that moment have been lying there in the snow, if only to give those fine chaps the feeling that we had shared their loss, as we had indeed shared the risk."

Howard Somervell

THE
EVEREST
POLITICS
SHOW

EXPEDITION DISPATCH
A BRIEFING AT THE MINISTRY

Footsteps on the Mountain Blog – Wednesday, 2ⁿᵈ of April 2014

A new joke is doing the rounds in Kathmandu.

How many Nepalese Ministry of Tourism officials does it take to change a light bulb?

Two. One to change the bulb and the other to issue a press release to the media.

There has been a flurry of strange announcements by the government in the last few months about rule changes on Everest. Climbers have to carry eight kilograms of garbage down with them. We have to attend a briefing to promote peace and harmony on the mountain; a ladder will be installed on the Hillary Step; everyone must climb with a Nepali guide; police will be stationed at Base Camp; permit fees have been 'reduced' (in fact, they've been increased slightly, but never let the truth get in the way of marketing).

Nobody knows how many of these statements are serious or whether any will be enforced. Some have been mooted before. But the sheer number leaves the impression that if you string all the garbage coming out of the Ministry together, there will be enough to make a rope ladder all the way up the Hillary Step to the summit and down the other side into Tibet.

We're not sure why all these statements have been coming, but the feeling is that the government believes that Everest's image has been tarnished by all the negative media coverage that accompanied last year's fight between Ueli Steck and a team of Sherpas. They're keen to let people know they're in control of the situation.

In fact, these announcements have had precisely the opposite effect. The press have tucked in to a feast of negative stories. If you threw Rupert Murdoch's bloated carcass into a paddling pool full of sharks there wouldn't be a bigger feeding frenzy. Right or wrong, the government appears to be in as much control as Peter O'Toole with a crate of Mount Everest Whiskey.

Yesterday we attended our much-publicised briefing at the Ministry of Tourism. I would love to say things are now much clearer, but if anything, they're muddier.

A briefing to 'promote peace and harmony'?

'They're going to tell us not to fight the Sherpas. It's just a formality,' our expedition leader Phil Crampton quipped beforehand.

We assumed the fight had prompted the rule changes, but in fact an entirely different incident seems to have annoyed them just as much, if not more. Last year, a commercial client called Dan Hughes, climbing with the British mountaineering operator Jagged Globe, did a live television broadcast for the BBC on the summit. Apparently this requires a special permit that he didn't have.

Although Phil is leader of the Altitude Junkies' joint expedition to Everest and Lhotse, he won't be climbing Lhotse, so my name is listed as leader on our Lhotse climbing permit. At one point during yesterday's briefing one of the officials looked at me and said:

'So, Mr Mark, you are British? No BBC broadcasts like last year.'

'Yes, I'm British, so obviously I must work for the BBC,' I didn't say (it didn't seem the right moment for sarcasm).

The briefing threw up a confusing mass of rules, some of which seemed fine, and others which seemed extraordinary. I don't know which ones I need to take seriously, and many were lost in translation. The first official spoke to us in English so heavily accented we could understand little of what he was saying. We nodded politely. The second official spoke better English but rushed through a series of PowerPoint slides full of long paragraphs of text, and we had no hope of keeping up with all of them.

All news we broadcast from camp has to be passed to the Ministry first. Really? How about all the blogs, tweets, Facebook posts and emails we have no control over? We're not allowed to unfurl commercial banners on the summit, but how about all the climbers who are part funded by sponsorship and expected to produce a summit photo with their sponsor's logo?

'They tell us that stuff every year,' Phil said to me afterwards.

There are two rules that are definitely new, but neither seems to be well thought through. When we leave Base Camp to climb through the Khumbu Icefall we're supposed to sign out at the new Base Camp police check post. It sounds like a good idea in theory – if a major incident occurs, somebody knows who's in camp and who's on the mountain – but in reality most people climb through the Icefall at night. Is there really going to be a police officer with a logbook at 2am flagging down every head torch that passes by?

The second rule concerns the new requirement to carry eight kilograms of trash off the mountain. This announcement received unusually positive media coverage, but nobody's sure how it's going to work. We'll all be carrying our own trash back down with us, but am I really going to be spending my time in the Western Cwm combing the glacier for other people's litter to take back with me, or will I be resting? It would be nice to think I'd do the former, but I can think of half a dozen reasons why I might not. Eight kilograms is a huge amount of extra weight to be carrying at high altitude.

After presenting us with *khata* scarves, the officials insisted we pose for a team photo. The many hangers-on in the room produced a flurry of cameras and we smiled politely as they posed alongside us.

Were they confusing us with Reinhold Messner or Ed Veisturs? I don't know. None of us took any team photos of our own.

I know the government officials are only doing their job, however strange it might have seemed to us. It was all very amiable in the end, but I definitely left the briefing more confused than when it started. Tomorrow I'm looking forward to hitting the Base Camp trail and enjoying the simple life again for the next few weeks.

DAY 1
THE START OF THE EVEREST TRAIL

Thursday, 3rd of April 2014 – Phakding, Nepal

It's seven o'clock in the morning and I'm standing on the tarmac at Kathmandu Airport with Ian, Margaret and Edita, waiting to board a helicopter to Lukla.

We can't believe our luck. My previous visits to Kathmandu's domestic terminal have involved long waits in a packed and dirty waiting room. Flights have often been delayed or cancelled due to the weather, and on one occasion I waited seven hours, only to be told to return the following day.

But flying by private helicopter is a different story to using one of the commercial aircraft. We arrived at 6.30am and were promptly ushered through security. We took a ride in a pickup truck to the opposite side of the runway where our helicopter was waiting.

Dorje Sherpa is with us. He is sirdar (or Sherpa leader) of the Altitude Junkies' joint expedition to Everest and Lhotse. He is a bit of a legend in the Sherpa heartland of Nepal's Khumbu region. We have all climbed with him on Manaslu and Everest, and he will be helping the clients on the Everest team this time.

Ian, Margaret, Edita and I have all climbed Everest before, and we don't intend to climb it again. This time we'll be attempting Lhotse, the fourth-highest mountain in the world. It's linked to Everest by the South Col, and the climbing route is the same for much of the way. For a long time I've dreamed of following in the footsteps of Tenzing, Hillary and the early pioneers. I have longed to climb through the towering ice of the Khumbu Icefall and into the Western Cwm. I yearn to climb higher, and see the features I have read about in so many books. Lhotse offers me that possibility.

We're ushered into the helicopter, and Dorje sits in the front while the four of us sit in a line on the back seat. Ian and I are sandwiched in the middle. Before we depart, Margaret and Edita spend five minutes waving iPads and smartphones around, taking selfies. Margaret has a video camera, and Edita hands her iPhone to a man standing outside to take a picture. He closes the door and takes a few steps back to get us all in the shot. For a moment Edita thinks he's going to do a runner with her phone, but all is well as he takes the photo and hands the device back to her.

The rotors crank into motion. At 7.15 we ease forward so gently that I barely notice we've left the ground. Within seconds we are flying high above the colourful concrete buildings of Kathmandu.

The rest of the forty-minute flight is not so enjoyable for me. I had only two hours' sleep last night, and I'm feeling hungover (it's the same old story when I'm in Kathmandu with Ian). The air is hazy, and a faint smell of fuel wafts through the open window as we cruise at altitude.

I'm relieved when we turn towards Lukla airstrip, visible through the haze on a jungle hillside above rice terraces. It's famous for its scary landing. The pilot must brake with all his might up a steep runway before his aircraft hits the mountain at the far end.

As we drop from the sky Edita lets out a gasp and grips

the edge of the seat next to me, as though in terror. But she too has done this flight a few times before, and I'm pretty sure she's joking.

Today our landing is straightforward. We pass across the runway before coming to rest on the helipad alongside it. My discomfort on the flight is forgotten when we see a man lying on a stretcher, waiting to be lifted onto the chopper for the flight back to Kathmandu. Yesterday we heard that a Sherpa broke his leg fixing ropes on the route through the Khumbu Icefall.

It's been a very bad start to the season. Another Sherpa from the Peak Freaks team suffered a pulmonary edema at Everest Base Camp. He died in hospital in Kathmandu yesterday. Several more helicopters have been diverted this morning to help with a rescue on Ama Dablam – a small but dramatic mountain rising above the Imja Khola Valley on the route to Base Camp. The diversions mean we must wait three hours for the rest of our team to arrive on separate flights.

We are a large team this year, with seven clients on Everest and five on Lhotse. Two of the clients have friends and wives trekking up to Base Camp with them. Then we have Dorje and Phil Crampton, our expedition leader. In all, sixteen of us will arrive by chopper this morning.

Dorje leads us up to a teahouse above the runway, and we spend the next few hours drinking black tea and coffee as we watch the flights come in to land. It's a dramatic setting. There is a steep drop into the Dudh Khosi Gorge, and forested hillsides rise on either side. Upstream to our right the pointed snow-capped peak of Nupla towers over the valley.

Helicopters come and go. Some fly in the direction of Kathmandu; others head up the valley to help with rescues. Some arrive to evacuate trekkers and climbers who have been taken ill.

By 11.30 all members of our team have arrived and we are ready to leave on the Everest Base Camp trail. We amble through the narrow, paved main street of Lukla and down the hillside beyond. The trail is busy. Several Everest teams are heading out today, including Peak Freaks, a large team from Alpine Ascents, and our Altitude Junkies team. Porters carry enormous loads to stock the many teahouses along the trail. It's not a wilderness experience – this part of the trail is a sprawl of villages. We pass in and out of pine forest, and don't have to walk far before we reach another teahouse.

The people are an annoyance, but the dzos pose a real menace. These yak-cow cross-breeds are used as beasts of burden. They show no consideration for other trail users as they trudge along, and they are difficult to overtake, even on the safer sections. Much of the trail contours around hillsides, with a precarious drop to the left into the Dudh Khosi Gorge. Passing dzos on an exposed section is a little dangerous. I get halfway through overtaking a train of them when I sense a giant horn prodding my rucksack from behind. I grab a tree trunk to prevent myself being shoved over a cliff, and a porter who is watching lets out a gasp.

It's a close shave. It would have been a stupid way to start (or end) my expedition when I have much greater perils ahead. But I am safe, and I respond with a nervous giggle to let him know I'm OK.

On another occasion I have to cross a narrow suspension bridge over a chasm. Some porters amuse themselves by setting the structure rolling from left to right. They walk with their feet wide apart and stamp the edges roughly as they cross. Behind them I feel my stomach lurch and I nervously grasp the handrails as I complete the crossing, while muttering *you fuckers* repeatedly under my breath. But it's all in good spirit and I reach the other side with the insides of my stomach still in place.

I'm not in good form this morning, thanks to last night's intemperance. I walk slowly, stopping often to take a drink and keep myself hydrated. But it's a short day, and at one o'clock I see Phil, our expedition leader, standing outside a teahouse in the curiously named village of Phakding. The teahouse, The Buddha Lodge, belongs to Dorje, and we'll be staying here tonight.

I've timed it well; it starts raining almost immediately. My teammates are sitting around an L-shaped table, drinking milk tea and peering at their phones. Many of them bought new handsets in Kathmandu, hoping to take advantage of the 3G connectivity promised by Nepalese telecoms company NCell. I find myself a seat between Jay and Kevin. My stomach rumbles uncharacteristically, and I try to persuade them they can hear the sound of thunder.

'Mark, do you know how to crack the password for the Wi-Fi?' Margaret asks me as she fumbles with her phone.

'Why don't you just ask Dorje?' I reply.

Ricardo roars with laughter. 'Mark knows how to crack the Wi-Fi. It involves shouting "Dorje, what's the password?"'

Ricardo is a Mexican-American part-time mountain guide and part-time musician. He funded his Everest climb by starting up a page on the crowdsourcing website GoFundMe, and received generous donations from previous clients and fans of his music.

'I raised over $30,000, and it blew my mind,' he says.

This fascinates Robert, an American businessman with his own motorcycle dealership.

'What, people just give you money to go climb Everest? What do they get out of it?'

'They get to read my dispatches, but mostly they are doing it out of kindness. I'm so touched by it all.'

Mountain guides and musicians are two professions which capture the imagination. Ricardo happens to be both. Somehow I don't think it's a method that will work for Robert.

'You should try it, Robert,' I urge him. 'Why not get in touch with all those people you sold motorbikes to? Perhaps they will remember you and give generously!'

Robert is posting his own Everest dispatches to a blog called *The World's Top Motorcycle Dealer*.

In the afternoon I snooze in my room. There is a forty-inch TV in Dorje's dining room, and other team members enjoy a screening of the IMAX *Everest* movie. I've seen it once before, and I know it's a better experience to watch it in a special IMAX cinema. I skip this showing, though it does have special significance: Dorje helped to carry the nineteen-kilogram camera used to make the film to the summit of Everest.

I scratch my head when I hear roars of laughter coming from downstairs. I don't remember the movie being especially funny, and in many ways it's quite the opposite. It was filmed in 1996, the year when eight people died in a storm – an episode made famous by journalist Jon Krakauer in his book *Into Thin Air*. Parts of the IMAX movie cover this tragedy, and I'm astonished that people are laughing.

But I later discover that after the movie they watched *The Inbetweeners*, a TV sitcom about sex-starved teenagers.

At dinner I ask our Chinese team member Mel about his afternoon. I expect him to express bewilderment about the choice of TV viewing. His English is good, but not perfect, and there have been one or two confusing moments recently. In Kathmandu I asked him what he did for a living, and he replied 'I'm an actor'.

'You're an actor – wow!' I said. 'Do you do movies or stage?'

He looked at me like I was an imbecile.

'What?'

'Do you act in movies or at the theatre?' I replied, miming a rising curtain as best I could.

'What?' he said again.

It was only later I found out that he had said 'I'm an architect', not 'I'm an actor'.

When I ask what he was up to this afternoon he looks at me mysteriously. I repeat my question more slowly, but before I finish he reaches into his pocket and produces his iPhone. He shows me a photograph of a beautiful pencil sketch he drew of Phakding's main street. Mountains rise behind teahouses and pine trees etched in striking grey lines.

'Well, you've trumped all these people,' I say. 'They spent the afternoon watching puerile British comedy.'

After dinner I manage to find cricket on the telly. Fellow Lhotse climber Louis is South African, and a big cricket fan like me. We stay up watching for an hour or so, and are surprised when Robert stays up with us.

'I didn't think Americans liked cricket?' I say.

Robert nods at the TV. 'Who's the guy in the cowboy hat?'

'That's the umpire,' I say, shaking my head. Then after a pause I add: 'And it's a sun hat.'

DAY 2
MY KINGDOM FOR A HORSE

Friday, 4th of April 2014 – Namche Bazaar, Nepal

We leave Phakding at 7.45 for another short walk up the trail to Namche Bazaar, the capital of Sherpa Khumbu. Although our large group starts out together, we're soon strung out, passing through villages and forest at our own pace.

I'm always a slow plodder while acclimatising, so I'm not surprised when I drop to the back of the group and amble along on my own. Phil passes me at a canter early on. He tells me he needs to get to the front to slow Ian and Kevin down. I've climbed and trekked with Ian on many occasions, so I already know he's a bit of a boy racer, but I haven't climbed with Kevin before.

Kevin knows both Edita and Mel from one of Phil's expeditions to Manaslu, two years ago. On that occasion a huge avalanche uprooted their tents and tossed them several metres down the mountain – while they were still inside. They survived unharmed, but several other teams were not so lucky. Eleven people died, and the incident was followed by a media outcry about commercial expeditions on 8,000m peaks, claiming that inexperienced climbers were to blame for the tragedy.

It was a traumatic experience that caused them to think

12

carefully about whether to continue. The team was divided; around half of them, including Mel, decided to go home. Edita was one of those who chose to stay, and later in the season she reached the summit. For Kevin, the mountain gods made the decision on his behalf. He lost a boot in the avalanche, and could not have continued if he wanted to.

It sounds like Kevin could do with losing a boot on this occasion, too. Ian tells me later that he didn't have a hope in hell of keeping up with him.

I walk in shade for a short distance and cross a long steel suspension bridge to the other side of the river. Phakding sprawls along the trail for two or three miles, but beyond the bridge I pass into pine groves again.

The sun comes up from behind the mountains. Beside another small community of teahouses, I stop to put on sun cream and remove a layer. The scenery is dramatic. Pine forests are wedged between sheer rock faces, and the Dudh Khosi River crashes a route far beneath us, yet it's no wilderness – many villages with tourist lodges are crammed along the trail. The spaces between are still largely pine forest, but they are becoming swallowed up as more teahouses are built.

There are always slower people on a busy route like this. A steep trail rises and falls above the valley in broad staircases hewn into rocky cliffs. Rarely do I walk for longer than a minute in solitude before catching up with someone else. Despite my ambling pace, most of the other travellers are actually slower than me. Porters walk with giant baskets piled high with crates of beer and soft drinks. Large trekking groups only move as fast as their slowest member. They form bottlenecks, and while I prefer to amble, I have no choice but to increase my pace to get past them.

I stop frequently to let trains of dzos and ponies pass

the other way. Keen to avoid a repeat of yesterday's near-accident, I find a convenient perch on a rock and wait until they have all passed by.

After a while I catch up with Margaret and Edita. They are walking at a similar pace to me, so I end up walking with them for much of the way. Margaret walks in silence with iPod headphones in her ears, while Edita is more inclined to slow down and talk when the trail is not too steep. She also reveals a penchant for photobombing. I drop back to take a photo of them silhouetted against a backdrop of mountains as they cross a high footbridge. Edita realises what I'm doing and waves at me as she crosses, trying to ruin my photo by walking in a peculiar fashion.

We pass a bewildering number of checkpoints, and must register our details at every one. In a layby in the middle of nowhere, there is a trekking checkpoint run by the Trekking Agencies' Association of Nepal (TAAN). Next we reach the Sagarmatha National Park Office in the village of Monjo. A short distance beyond we pass an army checkpoint in the forest. Here the officer tries to keep my trekking permit, and I have to rip it out of his hands. Quite what he expects me to do at the next checkpoint without my permit isn't clear. Before the day is out, we pass a police checkpoint near Namche Bazaar.

At least this final checkpoint provides some light relief. Margaret is sixty-four years old, but she has summited Everest from both sides and shows no sign of retiring. Back home in Perth, Australia, she is known as Supergran, but she doesn't look anything like sixty-four, or a gran. The police officer looks confused when he reads our permit and copies down her details. When he gets to her age he pauses, looks up at her, pauses again, then finally scribbles down forty-six.

The final section into Namche Bazaar involves a long

ascent of about 500m. It climbs through pine forest from the junction of the Dudh Khosi and Bhote Khosi rivers. Most of the trail is in shade, but plenty of sun beams through the trees, and it's hot and dusty.

Edita and Margaret cross the Dudh Khosi on a suspension bridge, with Khumbila as a backdrop

I'm prepared for it, and I trudge upwards, taking care not to get out of breath. At one point I pass a lady who does not seem cut out for high-altitude trekking. She is sweating profusely and struggling for breath, but she battles on.

'How are you doing?' she gasps at me as I pass.

'I'm doing OK. Not far to go now,' I say, by way of encouragement.

'You're doing good,' she replies.

'Thank you, you're very kind.' I fail to suppress a laugh. I hope she isn't offended.

A short while later the tables are turned when a guide from another group races past me. *Venus in Furs* by the Velvet Underground echoes from his iPhone. The first I know of it is when I hear Lou Reed's voice droning in my ear.

'I am tired, I am weary, and I could sleep a thousand years.'

This time I roar with laughter.

'Great motivational music!' I shout in the guide's wake. But he's already several metres beyond me and I don't know whether he hears.

Shortly before Namche, we meet Kevin waiting beside the trail to direct us to the teahouse. It's a kind gesture, but there's something missing. It's common in Nepal for the kitchen crew to meet their trekkers with a pot of hot lemon. I'm disappointed when Kevin can only provide us with directions.

'Where's the hot lemon, Kevin?'

'Damn it, I forgot!'

We reach our teahouse, The Nest at the bottom end of Namche, at midday.

It isn't such a successful day for everyone. Louis the South African is an Everest summiteer. He's the fifth member of the so-called 'Dream Team', the name Phil has given to the five of us who are climbing Lhotse. Louis, Ian, Margaret, Edita and I have all climbed Everest.

Louis is here with his wife Dia, who is trekking as far as Base Camp. We are not surprised that we have reached the teahouse before them. We assume that Dia, who has not trekked at high altitude before, is wise enough to take her time.

But Phil receives an unexpected text message from Robert, who has stopped to wait for them with his friend Scott. Scott is a surgeon who has also just come for the Everest Base Camp trek.

Louis struggling. We've ordered a horse to carry him to Namche.

Phil's reply is terse.

Is this a joke?

We learn that Louis has picked up some kind of illness, and that he went to the toilet an astonishing forty times last night (I have a feeling this number may be exaggerated). Now he is suffering from severe dehydration, and struggling to walk a hundred metres without stopping to vomit.

Phil is as sympathetic as ever. He spends the afternoon thinking up jokes to greet Louis with on his arrival.

'Making an ass of yourself again I see, Louis.'

Or an old one:

'You had a bad cough this morning. Have you been feeling a little horse this afternoon?'

He's disappointed when Robert sends another message to say they've been unable to hire a horse. Instead, Robert and Scott resort to increasingly bizarre methods to get Louis up the trail.

Scott unpacks his medical kit, and gives Louis a dexamethasone injection to provide him with an energy boost. This steroid is most frequently used as the drug of last resort for climbers who are collapsing with exhaustion.

Next Robert tries short-roping him, another old mountaineering technique in which a struggling climber is helped by towing them down a mountain. Usually a two- to three-metre length of Prusik cord is used to link rescuer and victim, but a porter is carrying Robert's climbing equipment, so he tries to use his belt instead. Back at the teahouse, we imagine Robert's trousers falling to his ankles as Louis staggers behind. We roar with laughter.

Dorje catches up with them and lends a hand by giving

Louis an extra push. Meanwhile Dia walks alongside, giving Louis every encouragement.

'Come on, Louis, you've climbed Everest. Stop being so pathetic!'

They reach Namche at three o'clock, and Louis begins the long process of rehydrating. His stomach bug will go away in a few hours. As long as he replenishes the water and salts that his body has lost in the last day, he'll be fine.

So much for the Dream Team. Ian and I now look like a pair of superstar athletes, but Ian fails to take this responsibility seriously. While I spend the afternoon snoozing and catching up with my diary, he goes out for a wander around the village. He returns a couple of hours later with a list of all the bars he's been able to find. He insists that we have to visit all of them later tonight.

At dinner I sit opposite Kevin and Edita. I ask them what it was like to live through the avalanche on Manaslu in 2012, which killed eleven people. They were at Camp 2 when it struck, and the tail of the avalanche rolled them around as it wafted past. Camp 3 was located 400m up a snow slope above them. It was directly in line, and was wiped out.

Kevin was sharing a tent with Phil. 'He made us sleep in the topmost tent "in case anything happened",' Kevin says. 'Before we went to sleep he brought his boots inside to keep them warm. He suggested I did too, but I thought "oh, they'll be all right out there".'

The following morning one of his boots vanished under the snow, never to be seen again. Its loss caused him to abandon the expedition.

Edita had just woken up and put the stove on for a brew when they heard a distant rumble high above them.

'I think that's an avalanche,' her tent mate Mila said, nervously glancing around at the walls of their shelter.

A few seconds later the blast threw them into the air

and they found themselves rolling down the slopes inside their tent.

'It must have been pretty terrifying,' I say.

'Not really,' Edita replies. 'It was over so quickly we didn't have time to think about it. As soon as we landed my worry was that we might be buried under so much snow we would suffocate inside the tent. I was so relieved when I opened the zip and could see the stars above us.'

In some respects they were lucky, but they agree that Phil had made a wise decision the previous night. He could see the slopes above Camp 2 were laden with fresh snow and a potential avalanche hazard. Their camp was protected behind a large crevasse, and they intended to retreat to Base Camp first thing that morning.

A 300m chunk of ice broke off a serac high above Camp 3, setting the entire slope below it into freefall. The climbers at Camp 3 took the brunt of it, but had they read the signs like Phil they would not have been there that morning.

'Remind me not to share a tent with either of you guys,' I say. 'Hopefully nothing like that's going to happen this time.'

Louis has recovered sufficiently for Phil to make more jokes at his expense. Dia asks whether it's possible to get some laundry done at the teahouse here in Namche.

'Yes, but they heard what happened today and won't take Louis's underwear,' Phil says.

When it's time to take our breakfast order for tomorrow he asks Louis whether fifteen slices of toast will be enough for him to keep some of it down.

By the end of dinner Ian has been drinking Tuborg beer for much of the afternoon and is feeling quite tired. I manage to round up eight people for our pub crawl, but the evening ends before eleven o'clock in only the second bar.

Both bars are strangely quiet. Are we early or late in the trekking season? I wonder. Or perhaps Namche is not the bustling metropolis I believed it had become.

DAY 3
THE SEEDY SIDE OF NAMCHE

Saturday, 5th of April 2014 – Namche Bazaar, Nepal

We've climbed to an altitude of 3,400m in just two days. Today we have a rest day, which we spend acclimatising in Namche Bazaar.

On a good day the Sherpa capital is one of the most spectacularly sited villages anywhere in the world. It lies in a bowl in the hillside hundreds of metres above the Bhote Khosi Gorge. Row upon row of multi-storey stone teahouses are piled on top of one another, stretching up the hillside, and bookshops, bakeries, outdoor clothing stores and trekkers' lodges line the narrow streets. On a clear day the 6,187m snowcap of Kongde Ri towers over everything on the opposite side of the valley. The village is home to the Sagarmatha Pollution Control Committee (SPCC), the organisation who regulate the environment in the Khumbu region. There is a helipad and a Sherpa cultural museum on top of the hill.

Today is not a day for taking sightseeing photos. A dull grey cloud floats low overhead, obscuring Kongde and banishing any blueness from the sky. The Statue of Liberty could be sitting on the hillside opposite for all we can see of it.

Louis looks a lot better this morning after his toilet

adventures yesterday. Last night we watched the T20 world cup cricket semi-final in a bar, and at breakfast I am unable to resist telling him that Dale Steyn was producing as much crap with the ball as he was out of his arse.

After breakfast I walk up the hill into the main part of Namche. Narrow streets are crammed with bookshops, trekking lodges, and stores selling outdoor clothing. I bump into Phil, who tells me the rest of the team are at a bakery down the hill. I follow him there, and find Margaret and Edita sitting at a table, drinking coffee and tapping away on their iPads. Edita tells me some of the others are sitting in another bakery opposite.

'How do you know?' I ask.

'One of them has posted on Facebook.'

Times have changed since I was last here. I go across the road, and sure enough, Kevin is sitting at a table not twenty metres away from Edita. He is also tapping away on his iPad. He doesn't notice me arrive, so I pull up a chair and sit down opposite without saying a word. When he glances up he looks shocked.

'That's freaky,' he says.

He shows me his iPad, and I see that he's been reading a page from my blog.

'What are you doing reading that shit?' I ask.

We go back across the road and join Margaret and Edita for coffee and chocolate cake. One by one the rest of the team join us as Phil notices them walking past outside. Most pull out smartphones or iPads and try to connect to the Wi-Fi.

I seem to be the only person in the group not bothered about checking emails or Facebook. I know I'm going to sound like an old fogey, but for me, an expedition is an opportunity to get away from the modern world for a few weeks.

Or so I like to think, but I get sucked in too. Later that

afternoon I spend an hour and a half in an internet café next door to the bakery. I try to write and send a blog post on a treacle-slow internet connection. If this isn't unpleasant enough, I'm forced to listen to a Sherpa issuing a stream of profanities in fluent English. He sits behind a counter near the door, while I sit among a bank of computer terminals a few metres away. The phone rings and he picks it up. He grunts a few terse responses as he listens to a voice on the other end of the line.

'Fuck you, why are you hassling me, man?' he says repeatedly.

It's quite some time before I realise he is talking to a western woman. When I do, it happens in a way that makes me feel quite sick.

'I will beat you, man,' he says. 'I have beaten other women, and I will beat you, too.'

And then a short while later he says: 'I just want your money, man. I want your fucking money.'

A Sherpani woman comes in to rebuke him. She also speaks in fluent English, and I assume she does so for my benefit. I am their only customer and I can hear every word.

'This is a business phone. Why you not use your cell phone? You have been on phone for an hour and customers may be trying to call us.'

He ignores her and keeps talking. Perhaps he will beat her later too. Namche is in a beautiful setting, but it's no paradise. I'm glad when I finish what I need to do, pay up and leave.

There are nice people here too. In the evening I meet up with my friend Siling in the Irish pub. He is a Nepalese trekking guide whom I have travelled with many times. I saw him in Kathmandu a few days ago, but it didn't register with either of us that we would be in Namche at the same time. He was surprised when he bumped into Ian walking around the village earlier in the day. He is guiding three clients to Everest Base Camp, but they are feeling a little under the weather today, so he has a free evening.

He tells us that, despite the number of trekkers we overtook on the trail yesterday, the Khumbu region is quiet this year. He says this is mainly due to the poor reliability of flights to Lukla – the principal means for tourists to access the area. Low cloud causes frequent cancellations, and Siling says there were no flights either today or yesterday.

Some of the domestic airlines have a safety record comparable to Evel Knievel's. They do not maintain their planes to international standards, resulting in a number of fatal accidents on Twin Otter flights in recent years. Many of the aircraft have been decommissioned, so there is now a much smaller fleet. Insurance is also becoming an issue. Some travel insurance policies now have 'Lukla exemptions'.

Phil's decision to send us by helicopter is looking like a wise one. Ian explains that helicopters are able to fly in worse conditions than the Twin Otters. The planes need to be able to see the runway from several miles away to land safely. Helicopters can fly much closer, and hover while they look for a landing pad.

Siling says there is now talk of building a road all the way to the village of Surkhe, a short distance below Lukla. Currently it takes five or six days to trek there from the roadhead at Jiri.

It's quiet in the Irish pub. Kevin and Mel join us for a drink, but there are just two other small groups present. Afterwards, Siling, Ian and I go to one of only three other bars in Namche. It's called the Liquid Cocktail Bar, and we find it down an alleyway off the main street. This time we are the only customers, although this is partially explained by the choice of music. Gentle, cheesy, 80s pop is playing when we arrive, but I believe the staff overhear us being critical. Two tracks later they start playing thrash metal. Tuneless electric guitar chords punish our eardrums while a man barks 'you're gonna die, you're gonna die, you're gonna die' over and over again. I hope it's not an omen for our expedition.

We say our goodbyes to Siling and return to our teahouse, The Nest, at eleven o'clock. It's been a very late night for a trek in Nepal.

DAY 4
THE PLOT THICKENS

Sunday, 6ᵗʰ of April 2014 – Deboche, Nepal

We take an early breakfast and leave Namche Bazaar at
7.15 for the next leg of our journey. Louis is feeling a little
better this morning, but has taken the precaution of
sending his pack with a porter. Meanwhile his wife Dia,
who is trekking to Base Camp with us, carries her own
pack.

'Look at this,' Phil says as we prepare to leave. 'Louis
looks like a trekker while Dia looks like a climber.'

Ricardo is also feeling ill this morning, but he left it too
late to hire a porter and has to carry his own pack.

I catch up with Louis and Dia and walk behind them for
a while.

'Is it traditional in South Africa to get your wife to carry
your kit for you?' I ask.

Louis is embarrassed, and a little while later I see him
take the pack off Dia and carry it himself.

Above Namche the broad trail contours around a
hillside. We see a pair of Impeyan pheasants, the national
symbol of Nepal, prancing on a bank above us, their
iridescent plumage shimmering in the light. The trail
swings to the left and rejoins the Dudh Khosi Valley. For
the next few miles the view is spectacular as we contour

high above the river. There is forest below us, and the jagged outline of Lhotse rises in a haze of blue far ahead.

By the time we reach the village of Kjanjuma the cloud has lifted completely and it's a glorious day. I've been ambling at the back, taking many photographs, and when I catch up with the others they are sitting in the garden of a teahouse, swigging soft drinks. The mountain panorama is marvellous: Taboche Peak right above us and Lhotse to the east; Ama Dablam, Kangtega and Thamserku rising in a line across the valley. Thamserku is perhaps the most dramatic from this angle, an impossible shark's fin piercing the sky.

Edita searches for 3G on the trail above Namche Bazaar

People are making fun of Edita. She has her phone out, and stops to tweet and post photos to Facebook from time to time.

'Spot the blogger!' Phil says.

'Recognised by her mating call, "3G, 3G, 3G",' Kevin says.

As a fellow blogger I should probably be more sympathetic. But here among breathtaking mountains I have no wish to wander along with my phone in hand, looking for 3G connectivity. I'm happy to spend time looking for a great photo, and I will write about my experiences when I reflect upon them later in the day. But I scribble my diary on paper for posterity, and will hardly look at my photos until I get home. As for real-time status updates on social networking sites, these are ephemeral. Only a handful of people will see them if they happen to be online when I post. And they will soon be forgotten. It would be a shame to spend time tweeting if it takes something away from my enjoyment of the mountains.

Beyond Kjanjuma, Robert and Scott intend to leave us and head up the Gokyo Valley. They will cross a high pass, the Cho La, and rejoin us at Base Camp in a few days' time. I overhear Phil and Dorje suggesting they spend two nights in the village of Machermo to help with their acclimatisation.

'I don't want to worry you guys,' I say, 'but there was a yeti attack in Machermo a few years ago.'

I relate the story, which is alleged to have happened in the 1970s. A Sherpani was tending her yaks in a field behind the village when she was thrown to the ground by a seven-foot yeti, which then proceeded to assault her livestock. It hurled a calf across the field with its bare hands, and wrestled its mother to the ground by the horns. It was then said to have torn the yak's stomach open and sucked out its entrails.

I provide as much detail as I can, but Robert and Scott just respond with matching smirks. I don't think they believe me.

We drop steeply through rhododendron forests to the

bottom of the valley, then cross the Dudh Khosi River on another long footbridge. But all this height must be regained. For the next two hours we trudge back up the hillside to the forested ridge where Tengboche Monastery looks out towards Everest.

The trail is hot and dusty, and there is only brief respite when trees above the trail provide some shade. I plod upwards, drinking frequently. I'm prepared for this climb, having come this way twelve years ago. It's just as I remember it. Tengboche lies on a shoulder of Kangtega, a silver-saddled peak which provides a dramatic backdrop to the walk.

At Kjanjuma, Ricardo's illness was slowing him down, so Dia agreed to carry his pack for him. A strange instinct makes him take it back off her for this part of the walk. Halfway up the hill he meets an Argentine friend coming the other way, a fellow guide he has met frequently when they were both guiding on Aconcagua, South America's highest mountain.

'Thank God I took my pack back,' he says afterwards. 'I would never have lived that one down if he saw Dia carrying it for me.'

We reach the colourful Tengboche Monastery at eleven o'clock. It's very busy. A group of Sherpas are playing volleyball, and a few people sit outside a bakery drinking coffee. A large teahouse stands opposite the monastery.

We have our first view of Everest, a giant black pyramid directly in front of us. The summit of Lhotse has disappeared behind a plume of cloud to its right. Khumbila, the mountain across the valley which stands sentinel over Tengboche, is also hidden by cloud. Khumbu-Yul-Lha is the protector god for the whole of the Khumbu region, and Khumbila is his home. It's the most holy of mountains, and it's forbidden for anyone to climb it.

Tengboche's ridge overlooks a confluence of rivers. To the north the Dudh Khosi River, which we've been following most of the way from Lukla, climbs up to the Gokyo Valley. I explored this beautiful valley in 2009, where a series of picturesque lakes nestle beneath Cho Oyu's enormous South Face. To the north-east the Imja Khola Valley continues towards Everest, and this is the direction we'll be taking tomorrow.

The speedsters Phil, Kevin, Ian and Jay have been here a while. They are enjoying a beer outside the bakery when we arrive. We continue over the other side of the ridge, dropping through rhododendron forests. Ten minutes later we reach the Rivendell Lodge, our overnight stop among trees in the small community of Deboche.

We leave our bags in our rooms and meet in the large upstairs dining hall, looking out at an Everest rapidly disappearing into cloud.

I am concerned because I saw Edita descend from Tengboche ahead of me, but she hasn't appeared at the lodge. We reached it sooner than expected and I'm sure she must have shot past and continued down the valley. Margaret is just as sure Edita must have stopped at the monastery, and is not concerned. Edita turns up half an hour later. She tells us she walked a little further down the trail after finding there was no 3G at the lodge.

As the afternoon passes, the Rivendell Lodge lives up to its name by disappearing into a thick Tolkienesque mist. We can see little more than a few metres out of the window.

At dinner time Phil tells a story that causes me to gape in shock. It follows a conversation about Sherpas – some of ours are climbing up to Camp 2 today, where they plan to rope off a section of the Western Cwm for our tents.

'Will this work?' I ask. 'Or are we going to climb up there to find people camped in our spot?'

'Sherpas will take notice of it,' Phil replies. 'Western climbers may ignore it and camp there, but if they do the Sherpas won't be happy.'

We talk about the fight at Camp 2 last year, when a pair of well-known European climbers, Ueli Steck and Simone Moro, clashed with Sherpas who were fixing ropes on the Lhotse Face.

There is an unwritten rule among the commercial operators on Everest that everyone should stay off the mountain when the Sherpas are fixing ropes. The two Europeans were unaware of this rule, and last year, as the rope-fixing team made their way up the face, Steck and Moro climbed alongside them. The pair were unroped, and their action hurt the pride of the Sherpas. When the climbers moved above them and kicked down some ice, an altercation took place.

The Italian, Simone Moro, was reported to have used some colourful Nepali words that he is unlikely to have learned in a language class. The Sherpas threw down their tools in protest and descended to Camp 2 to complete the job another day. When the two Europeans returned to Camp 2, an angry Sherpa mob confronted them. The mob were armed with rocks and knives, and the two Europeans had to beat a hasty retreat to Base Camp.

'Did you hear about our little incident at ABC [Advanced Base Camp] last year?' Phil says.

I shake my head.

'A South American climber came up to our camp shouting "One of you motherfuckers has shit in our toilet!" I calmed him down and explained that we had toilets of our own for people to use. I asked him not to swear in front of the Sherpas as they find it disrespectful. "I'm telling you, one of your fucking team shit in our toilet," he repeated. I asked him again to be polite in front of the Sherpas, or I couldn't be responsible for what happened.

But he carried on effing and blinding in front of us.'

My mouth hangs open in astonishment as Phil relates the next part of the story. Believing that he was accusing them of using his toilet, the Sherpas confronted him in a manner echoing the Ueli Steck incident. They used physical force and the South American climber was made to apologise. Sherpas I know well, and have never known to be anything other than polite and helpful, behaved in a way that surprises me greatly. Phil tends to avoid controversy and often takes on the role of peacemaker, but in this story he comes across as partially complicit.

'I'm telling you, the Sherpas don't like people being disrespectful,' he says.

These incidents leave an unpleasant taste in the mouth. I don't know whom to sympathise with, if anyone. Violence is never an answer for anything. On the other hand, to be rude and abusive in a place where the law doesn't stretch is also asking for trouble.

I look at Margaret and Edita, both of whom were at ABC last year.

'Is this true?'

'It's true. I wrote about it,' Edita says.

'This happened a couple of days before the Simone incident, and on the north side of Everest, where it's much quieter,' Phil adds. 'I was pretty relieved no one got to hear about it when that all kicked off in the media.'

DAY 5
BIRTHDAY PEANUTS

Monday, 7ᵗʰ of April 2014 – Dingboche, Nepal

It's Phil's birthday today, and at breakfast everyone sings *Happy Birthday*. I don't join in myself, for the simple reason that Phil doesn't appear to enjoy being serenaded. In fact, he looks as sick as a parrot, and I find the expression on his face so funny that I roar with laughter for the entire song.

Everest and Lhotse are visible again across the camping ground in front of the lodge. The sun touches the front yard just as we leave at 7.15. It's a short morning walk up to our next lodge at Dingboche, but these three hours are the best I've spent in a long time. The trail is not especially busy, but the scenery is as breathtaking as anything I will ever see.

I came this way in the opposite direction five years ago when I returned from Island Peak. It was a total whiteout, snow fell for much of the walk, and I could see virtually nothing of the surrounding countryside. Today I see what I was missing, and my camera is rarely out of my hand.

We start with a gentle descent through thick and gloomy rhododendron forest. We reach the valley floor and cross over the Imja Khola River on a short footbridge. On the north bank the trail climbs again to the village of Pangboche. The sun hangs high over the armchair shape of

Ama Dablam, providing only a hazy view, but up ahead the black fortresses of Everest and Lhotse are clear and bright, bounded by the battlements of the Nuptse ridge.

I walk at the back with Dia and Louis for much of the way. This is Dia's first time in Nepal and she seems to be enjoying it even more than I am.

Beyond Pangboche the broad trail winds high above the river, lined with chortens and mani walls. These are Buddhist symbols, the first a bell-shaped monument and the second a line of slabs. They are inscribed with the mantra *om mani padme hum*, a phrase whose literal translation – praise to the jewel in the lotus – is obscure, but full of significance. According to tradition we have to pass to the left-hand side of them, ensuring the inscribed prayers are read the right way. These diversions sometimes take us up steep banks on narrow trails.

Across the valley to our right Kangtega changes from a silver saddle to a narrow needle. Eventually we see another slender peak behind it, and I'm unsure which is the true summit.

After climbing above 4,000m I reach a broad, dry plateau strewn with boulders and scrubby juniper bushes. Here I catch up with Louis, Dia, Margaret, Edita and Ricardo. Kangtega is behind us now, and every bit as spectacular as Lhotse in front. Everest has disappeared behind the Nuptse ridge.

We take it in turns to pose for photos. I get out my mini tripod and set up a group shot of the six of us using my camera timer, an exercise that often produces giggles when I fail to get into the shot in time.

Beyond the plateau the trail branches either side of a small hill. The left branch leads to Pheriche, where there is a small hospital and a helipad, while the right branch drops down to the river, crosses over, then leads steeply up again on the right side of the hill.

The view is magnificent. I have only ever been here in a whiteout, but I recognise the parting of the ways from the features on my map. Although Louis, Margaret and Edita have all been this way too, in much better conditions, they are content to let me lead. I stride confidently ahead and keep turning around to film them coming up behind me. Every time they reach me, instead of continuing onwards, they stop and wait for me.

'You are the leader on our Lhotse climbing permit,' Edita points out. This is true – on the expedition paperwork one of us had to be designated leader, since Phil himself will be climbing Everest rather than Lhotse. It fell to me to take on the role, despite the fact that the only thing I'm likely to lead them on is a merry dance.

'But you've all been here more than I have,' I reply.

We cross another plateau, crest a rise and see Dingboche across an open area between hills. As we begin our descent to the village I turn to film them again, only to find Margaret pointing her own video camera at me as she walks.

'Ahead of us is the famous blogger Mark Horrell,' I hear her say. We've bumped into a few people over the last few days who have admitted to reading my blog, and Margaret always finds this funny.

'Are you getting your own back?' I shout back at her. 'And here comes the famous Supergran,' I say to my camera as she approaches.

At 10.15, we reach the Mountain Paradise Lodge at the far end of the village. It's another spectacular setting here in Dingboche. Ama Dablam rises right above us, its twin summits looking very different from any other angle I've seen them from. Its sheer north face now looks horrendous, a giant wall of rock draped in ice. These lily-white sheets are marked with stripes, the telltale sign of avalanches hurtling down its surface.

'You were walking so fast at the end,' Edita says as we settle into the dining room. 'We thought you must have taken some pill.'

There is a mischievous glint in her eye, and I clock what she is talking about.

'Don't tar me with the same brush as Robert.'

Robert once admitted to taking Viagra on a climb, and he said it helped him significantly. Last year he even encouraged Margaret to try it during their Everest expedition, but she declined.

'I know Robert says it helps him to get up,' I say.

The lodge is comfortable, and there are windows across two walls of the dining room, providing a grandstand panorama of Ama Dablam and Kangtega. But the furniture seems to have been designed for lighter people than us. I sit down next to Margaret on a plywood bench and hear it crack beneath me, causing her to roar with laughter. Then Phil sits on a plastic chair and it breaks. He stands up just in time, but this sets me off laughing too. Despite watching us destroy her furniture, the lady owner of the teahouse doesn't seem to mind, and she joins in with the laughter.

After a short snooze in the somewhat darker bedroom that I share with Ian, I return to the dining room at six o'clock. The others are already celebrating Phil's birthday; I see empty tins of Tuborg and Everest beer on the table. At the end of dinner Dorje comes over with a proud expression on his face. He announces that we have drunk the whole village out of Tuborg. But if we want any tomorrow night, they can send someone over the hill to Pheriche to see if there's any there.

I arrive to dinner carrying my copy of *The Ascent of Rum Doodle*, W.E. Bowman's great comic novel about an expedition to a fictional mountain. Mel has picked it up before I can start reading it, and by the time our dinner arrives he is already on the second chapter. When I tell him he is welcome to hold on to it as long as he carries it up to Base Camp with him, he gives it to Edita. By the end of dinner she has passed it on to Ricardo, who says he was looking all over Kathmandu for a copy.

Luckily we have finished eating when Phil decides to tell his peanuts story.

'I think it was 2008. I was sitting on the South Col preparing for my summit push when Tim Rippel of Peak Freaks put his head into my tent. He asked if I wanted a bag of peanuts that he didn't want to carry down with him. They go down well, and by the time we leave for the summit I've eaten most of the bag. We go up, summit, and come back down again, but by the time I get back to the South Col my stomach's feeling a bit dodgy. I decide to continue all the way down to Camp 2 in the Western Cwm where I know we have a toilet tent. When I get there I'm desperate to go, but find I've got the worst constipation you can imagine.

'I hear over the radio that one of my clients is having problems higher up the mountain. I'm in no position to go and help him. I'm having problems of my own just trying to shit, so I go over to the Himex tent and ask Phurba Tashi if he can help me. He agrees right away and begins getting ready.'

Phurba Tashi Sherpa is an Everest legend who has climbed the mountain twenty-one times. It's a record he shares with the equally legendary Apa Sherpa.

'You asked Phurba Tashi to help you go to the toilet?' I say in astonishment.

'No, with the fucking rescue, you idiot,' Phil says. 'It was a bit of an epic, but the guy survived. Meanwhile I'm struggling so hard in the toilet tent that I pass out. I fall forward with my pants around my ankles, and when I wake up there's a group of people taking photographs.'

'Hang on a moment,' Kevin says, brow furrowed.

'What's the significance of the peanuts?'

'I think that's what blocked him,' I reply.

'I realise there's only one thing for it. I'm going to have to unblock myself by hand,' Phil continues. 'I go to the kitchen tent and ask our chef Jangbu if we have any laxatives in the med kit. "Do we have any lubricant?" I ask. He goes into the store tent and returns with a bottle of oxygen. "What am I supposed to do with that?" I say. Then he produces a tin of tuna. "That might just do the trick." I take it to the toilet tent, and with a bit of prodding around I'm able to get my bowels working again.'

This time everybody around the table is looking on with open mouths. If last night's story had shocked me, I have no idea what to say this time. Two things I won't be trying at Base Camp are peanuts and tuna.

We turn in at 9.30, not long after Phil's peanuts story, but before I fall asleep, I overhear voices through the plywood wall that separates our rooms. There is more laughter, and I hear Ricardo quoting passages from *The Ascent of Rum Doodle* to Kevin. It makes me smile.

DAY 6
ACCLIMATISING ON POKALDE

Tuesday, 8th of April 2014 – Dingboche, Nepal

There are a few niggling illnesses at breakfast this morning. Ian has the *Khumbu cough*, the dry high-altitude rasp that he seems to suffer from on every expedition. He apologises for keeping me awake all night, but I wore my earplugs and hardly noticed. Kevin has a stomach problem and Dia is also feeling ill. She doesn't emerge for breakfast. Phil produces the medical kit and hands out throat lozenges, ciprofloxacin and aspirin.

'Dia wants to know if you have any Viagra,' I say.

Louis laughs louder than anyone else, though it seems to me a nervous sort of laugh.

It's supposed to be a rest day today, but after breakfast I set off up the hill behind our lodge for a modest hike that lasts longer than I anticipate.

The main trail to Lobuche slants across the hillside to a mini pass bedecked with Buddhist prayer flags and stupas. The sky is completely clear, and the sheer faces of Ama Dablam and Kangtega stare down at me across the valley. Both mountains look intimidating, but at the pass two equally impressive peaks appear to the west. They are Taboche Peak and Cholatse, a fiendish pair of snow-capped needles whose summits look severe. Sheer cliffs guard the lower sections of Cholatse. It looks to be the hardest peak I have seen in the Khumbu.

None of these peaks would be my cup of tea to climb, but they are indescribably beautiful, and it is a privilege to look at them from below.

Taboche Peak rises above Dingboche

It's a pleasant morning for an acclimatisation walk. I turn right and follow dozens of other people up a ridge. Some are trekkers, but most, like us, are climbers heading for Everest and Lhotse. When I arrived yesterday morning I had no idea so many people were staying in Dingboche.

The trail is steep and dusty. I plod up grassy slopes beside the path to avoid inhaling the clouds of dust kicked up by so many hikers. After an hour I have ascended 300m and overtaken the largest of the trekking groups. I find myself alone on the slope with only a few isolated figures above me.

Two of these are Ian and Caroline, a nurse from New Zealand with whom I climbed in Alaska last year. At the time I had no inkling she had ambitions to climb Everest. I was surprised when Phil contacted me a few months later asking for a reference.

'Hey, Horrell,' it read (Phil's prose is very similar to his speech). 'I got an email from this Kiwi chick asking if she can sign on to my Everest expedition. So I Googled her name to get her climbing experience, and discovered you climbed Denali with her.'

I must have talked about Altitude Junkies while we were on Denali. I was tempted to ask Phil for a commission for referring a client to him, but I knew what his response would be (the second word would have been 'off'). Instead, I gave him an honest assessment of Caroline's climbing skills. It must have been OK, because here she was.

I catch up with Caroline and Ian a short while later. Ian has pulled his buff over his face to avoid the dust. He has decided to descend, but Caroline is keen to continue.

I see Louis on the trail behind me. I head for a rocky sub-peak a short distance above us, and reach it by way of a gentle scramble over rocks. We meet Margaret and Edita on the summit.

After a great acclimatisation hike, it's eleven o'clock and we've climbed 700m to an altitude of 5,050m. None of us had any intention of climbing high when we set off. Edita doesn't even have any water, and only came up here looking for 3G. She didn't find it, but has no regrets, for the view is incredible.

Everest and Lhotse hide behind the mountain we are climbing, which turns out to be a trekking peak called Pokalde, but the giant black pyramid of Makalu has appeared in the distance to the east. Far beneath Makalu, tiny Island Peak is camouflaged against higher slopes behind it.

To the right of Makalu a series of fluted peaks and faces continue to the whaleback ridge of Baruntse and the less prominent Kali Himal. Ama Dablam, Kangtega, Taboche and Cholatse have remained visible all along, but up the valley to the north two more peaks have appeared. The steep snow ridge of Lobuche rises in the foreground, and the snow plateau of Cho Oyu stretches out behind it.

We stay on top for forty-five minutes, taking many photos and videos. I'm the only person who knows the names of all the peaks, so Margaret asks me to video the panorama for her with commentary in what she calls my 'beautiful British accent' (I have a slightly stupid Yorkshire accent, but she's Australian, so I can see her point).

The rest of the team are standing in front of me. I describe the mountains as Margaret asked, but I ruin her footage by making a series of inappropriate jokes as I pan the camera past each of them.

It takes just forty-five minutes to run down the dusty slopes back to Dingboche. Halfway down we meet Phil on his way up. He says he was concerned that Edita might discover an internet connection and end up missing lunch, so he came up to find her.

The sky has remained clear throughout the morning. It's been a perfect acclimatisation hike to a grandstand seat above this shining mountain amphitheatre, and I feel blessed.

At dinner I sit next to Margaret. This is her fifth Everest expedition in as many years (Lhotse counts in my book). She climbed on the south side in 2010 and 2011, reaching the summit at the second attempt. Then she joined us on the north side in 2012 but turned around at the Third Step. Last year she tried again from the north side and was successful.

That's four expeditions and two summits, from both

sides. Not bad for a grandmother. I ask her to compare north and south.

'The trek to Base Camp on the south side is very beautiful,' she says, 'and then you climb through the Khumbu Icefall. On the north side I didn't enjoy the drive to Base Camp. Nyalam and Tingri are not very nice places to stay, and the walk up from Base Camp to ABC is a bit boring. But above ABC the north side is beautiful.'

I ask her about the difficulties on summit day.

'On the north side you leave camp and begin climbing straight away through rocks, and it's hard. The only place you can relax is on the ridge between the Second and Third Steps. Everywhere else is very exposed. On the south side you begin by crossing the South Col. Then it is steep, but it is wide. Above the Balcony all the way to the South Summit the ridge is very wide. There are two ropes, but if you want to overtake people you can unclip very easily and get past. You cannot do that on the north side.

'Between the South Summit and the Hillary Step it is very exposed, but this section is short. On the north side you have the triangular face above the Third Step, which is much longer. It seems to go on for ever. The Second Step is much harder than the Hillary Step.

'On the south side you have a lot of ascent – nearly 1,000m from the South Col. But when I got back to Base Camp last year, I told Phil the north side is much harder than the south.'

It's a good summary, and makes me feel better about my eighteen-hour summit day on the north side, which I only just survived. One thing's for sure, though: whatever anyone says, neither side is easy.

DAY 7
THE GLARE OF THE KHUMBU

Wednesday, 9th of April 2014 – Lobuche, Nepal

It's another beautiful day. We take an early breakfast and leave Dingboche at 7.10 bound for Lobuche, a few hours up the main Khumbu Valley.

We climb slowly up to the pass we ascended yesterday morning. Beyond it, instead of heading up the ridge as we did on yesterday's acclimatisation walk, we descend over the other side onto a long plateau.

Almost immediately, a small group of us drops behind the others. Phil is keen to reach Lobuche in good time to ensure we have rooms at the Mother Earth Lodge. All the Everest climbers, and Ian, keep close on his heels as best they can. By the time I reach the pass they are already some distance across the plateau.

Meanwhile, Margaret, Edita, Louis, Dia, Dorje and I linger at the back in our own little group. We are four fifths of the Lhotse 'Dream Team'. While Louis may be walking more slowly to keep his wife Dia company, how do you explain the rest of us? Are the Everest climbers stronger than we are, or are they pushing themselves too hard? Does our greater number of 8,000m expeditions make us wiser, so that we are content to take it easy at this early stage?

For my part I want to enjoy this experience for as long as I can. I walk among truly breathtaking scenery – towering rock walls and shimmering horizons of ice – and I know we have only a short distance to travel to Lobuche. I am in no hurry to get there.

We are climbing out of the alpine zone now, into high-altitude desert. The plateau is dusty and brown, the only vegetation a few isolated patches of dwarf juniper. The trail drifts to the left of the plateau, and soon we are looking down into the Khumbu Valley and the village of Pheriche. This is the place we'll return to at the end of the expedition to catch helicopters back to Kathmandu. From here it looks like a small farming community in a flat valley, surrounded by stone-walled fields.

Across the valley the two impossible peaks of Taboche and Cholatse rise in sheer walls of ice-crowned rock. They remain our companions for the next couple of hours. As we move north they change shape, but at no point do they become any less frightening. I can see no feasible routes up for any but the most talented, bold and committed climbers. I'm none of those things.

The path keeps to the edge of the plateau, looking down on the valley to our left. Gradually we descend to join it and cross a bridge beneath a community of teahouses known as Dughla.

Just before we reach the buildings Dia tells me she has lost her sunglasses. She thinks it happened when she stooped to tie her shoelaces. The peaks around us are snow-capped only in isolated places, but with such a bright sun I'm worried about snow-blindness. When she tells me she thinks she lost them on the short section before the bridge, I insist we return and look for them.

I drop my pack and we walk back for about ten minutes, but we don't see them. Several porters and yakpas have passed us by. If any of them saw Dia's glasses lying on the trail it's likely they would have picked them up and pocketed them.

We return to the teahouses where Louis is waiting for us. I suggest to Dia she pulls her buff up over her face to form narrow eye slits. Though not as effective as sunglasses it will provide some measure of protection from the sun.

Margaret, Edita and Dorje have started a steep climb up to another pass, and are some distance ahead. They don't know why we have been delayed, but when I set off after them they stop and wait a short distance above.

'Are you OK?' Dorje says when I arrive.

'Dia has lost her sunglasses, so we went back to look for them.'

'You find them?'

I shake my head.

We stop for water and I take out my trekking poles to help me on the steep ascent ahead. Within five minutes Dorje has stopped a porter coming the other way and negotiated a price of 2,000 rupees (about $20 USD) for his sunglasses. Well, I say *negotiated*, but Dorje is a determined man and not someone to mess with. Most likely he just said 'you give me those for 2,000' and the porter didn't argue.

The sunglasses are a decent pair of Bollés, and Dia is happy again. We reach the pass, the Thok La, spanned by an archway of prayer flags. Passing underneath, we find ourselves in a memorial ground to climbers who have died on Everest (and other mountains). A bewildering number of stupas have been erected on a bank beside the trail. Stupas also line another short ridge 100m away.

Although I have never heard of most of the climbers, every so often I come across a name I recognise. Scott Fischer, who died during the *Into Thin Air* tragedy of 1996, has the biggest one. Pete Boardman has another, to go with the one he shares with Joe Tasker at Chinese Base Camp on the north side of Everest. Alex Lowe died in an avalanche on Shishapangma, but is remembered here too. Most poignant for me is the memorial to Shriya Shah-Klorfine. She was a desperately inexperienced Canadian climber who reached the top of Everest from the south side on 19 May 2012, but died of exhaustion on the descent. I ascended from the north side that day, and it's conceivable that I stood beside her on the summit, a few hours before her final breath.

We pause for a few reflective moments before continuing. We have only half an hour to walk to Lobuche, but those few minutes will live long in the memory. The valley flattens out and bends to the right. The snow crown of Lobuche East is high overhead, and we see the yellow tents of the Himex expedition camped beneath it. To acclimatise for Everest, they will be climbing this 6,119m trekking peak instead of passing through the Khumbu Icefall.

Pumori rises up like a giant church bell at the head of the valley in front of us. It's not quite perfectly symmetrical – it falls away in a gentler ridge to the right – but it still looks a very difficult climb. It has a reputation for being dangerously avalanche prone. Edita tells me she would like to climb it some day.

'Don't you think it's a beautiful mountain?' she says.

'So is K2,' I reply. 'But it wouldn't be my cup of tea.'

The valley opens out, with moraine ridges and glacial boulders on either side. At some point in the past the Khumbu Glacier must have extended all the way down here. Now we have just a few short sections of ice to cross. [Unbeknown to me the Khumbu Glacier does indeed extend this far down the valley. It is hidden behind the moraine ridge to my right.]

We reach Lobuche at 10.30. It's an inhospitable location

for a village, but a lovely setting for trekkers and climbers. The village consists of three large trekking lodges looking across the valley to the crinkled black fortress of Nuptse.

Pumori and Lingtren seen from near the Everest memorials

We have ascended to 4,900m, and the rooms of the Mother Earth Lodge are cold as hell, but the dining room is warm and insulated.

At dinner I have a conversation about waste management on Everest with Dia, Louis and Phil. Dia asks what arrangements have been made for disposing of rubbish. Phil explains that we'll be packing everything out, including all food packaging and human waste. The human waste is taken to a place where it can be turned into fuel (biogas).

'An awful lot of shit is produced. If you can imagine thirty Sherpas having two meals of dal bhat every day, you start to get the idea,' he says, a little unnecessarily.

Louis leans across the table and says something to Dia in Afrikaans.

'*'N ton se kak.*'

Phil and I look at each other.

'Did he just say "I don't suck cock"?' Phil says.

'That's what I heard,' I reply.

'*'N ton se kak,*' Louis says again, and we roar with laughter.

'*'N ton se kak,*' Dia says. 'It means "a ton of shit".'

'You means it's an actual phrase in Afrikaans, and not just some joke sentence?'

Louis says it again, and this time everybody round the table starts laughing. He spends the rest of the evening teaching us rude words in Afrikaans, but I've forgotten them by the time we go to bed.

DAY 8
PEACE AND SOLITUDE

Thursday, 10th of April 2014 – Lobuche, Nepal

We all seem to be carrying some sort of bug. Ian was wide awake most of the night coughing. I have a severe cold and have turned into a one-man snot factory. I've used up every square inch of my handkerchief and have to buy a whole extra roll of toilet paper just to sneeze into.

Phil left at 5.30 this morning to head up to Base Camp. One of our kitchen Sherpas, Karma Gjalje, has been sent back down to help at the lodge here.

We have a rest day in Lobuche, and I spend the morning walking along the ridge of moraine opposite the village. From the top I find myself staring down onto the Khumbu Glacier, dusted grey with moraine. There is a cold breeze up here, but in the moments when it dies, or when I gain shelter behind rocks, the air is still and I enjoy the total silence.

The scenery is too beautiful for words. For the next three hours I amble along the ridge towards Base Camp on my elevated perch, contemplating peace and solitude, and the wonder of the mountains. This truly is one of the most magnificent places on Earth. The white cone of Pumori, its wedge-shaped sister peak Lingtren, and smaller Khumbutse rise ahead of me. To my left a green valley divides me from rocky Lobuche East, with a vast hanging glacier beneath its summit. To my right I look across the silvery Khumbu Glacier to Nuptse's citadel.

Lobuche East rises above the community of teahouses at Lobuche

Twice I stop in the shelter of a rock and think about nothing at all in this haven of the mountain gods. When I turn around and wander back, the view is no less magnificent. Taboche and Cholatse tower over me in walls of ice-crowned rock. The fluted pinnacles and ridges of Kangtega and Thamserku rise more distantly at the end of the valley.

It's a dusty, sandy track. I have my buff pulled over my nose and mouth, but by the time I return to the Mother Earth Lodge I feel like I've swallowed a great many particles – whether dust or strands of my buff, it's all the same. I may well remain ill for a couple more days, but there is plenty of time to recover at Base Camp. In any case, I wouldn't have missed this walk for anything.

Subdued by illness, it's a quiet team in the Mother Earth Lodge this evening. They are sitting around the stove in the centre of the dining room when I come down an hour or so before dinner. I creep to a nearby table to read my book, but Ian notices me and buys me a beer.

It takes me a long time to drink it, and I'm not sure it was what I needed. Earlier in the afternoon I bought Margaret a beer too, but she was also feeling ill and Edita told her not to drink it. The beer sat on the table for quite a while. Eventually I noticed Edita drink it herself. Not everyone is quite so ill then.

DAY 9
ARRIVAL AT BASE CAMP

Friday 11th of April, 2014 – Everest Base Camp, Nepal

We leave for Base Camp just after eight o'clock. Just as we're leaving I see someone I recognise shout instructions to his porters from the neighbouring teahouse. It's David Hamilton, leader of the Jagged Globe expedition, with whom I climbed Muztag Ata in the Chinese Pamirs a few years ago. I also recognise one of his clients, Denis, and his assistant leader Chris Groves, from previous expeditions.

They are just leaving for Base Camp themselves, so I chat to them as we walk along. They stayed in Dingboche like we did. They tell me that afterwards they continued up the Imja Valley to Chukung, and came back over a high pass, the Kongma La. They will be well acclimatised by now.

It's a long time since I last saw Chris, when he led my first expedition to Aconcagua in 2005. Since then he has become one of Jagged Globe's top 8,000m peak leaders, though this is his first time on Everest. Jagged Globe have had a remarkable success rate recently. Every one of their clients reached the summit in each of the last two years. Chris is non-committal when I ask him whether he thinks it will happen this time.

It's another lovely walk, but the trail is bustling with

trekkers and climbers heading to Base Camp. The land becomes increasingly barren. As we approach Pumori, standing sentinel at the end of the valley, the grassy outcrops present at Lobuche give way to scree and boulders.

We ascend a steep bank, then drop down to Gorak Shep and the last few teahouses on the trail before Base Camp. The lodges stand beside a huge sandy area which, in 2009, hosted the world's highest cricket match.

We sit and drink Sprite in one of the teahouses while a group of Sherpas sit opposite sipping hot lemon. Dorje doesn't introduce them, and they watch us in silence. We have been there for ten minutes when I suddenly recognise one of them. It's Chongba, who stood beside me on the summits of both Manaslu and Everest. He will be climbing Lhotse with me too.

I rush over and give him a big hug and a warm handshake. He grins broadly, and I believe he may have recognised me earlier, but he said nothing. It says something of his character that we've shared such experiences, yet still he was reluctant to come over. It's no surprise. Many of the older Sherpas exhibit this behaviour, which we take to be humility (though I don't know whether this is true). The younger Sherpas are different. Most speak better English and are more confident with western clients.

'They are all Altitude Junkies,' says the teahouse owner as he walks past.

There is a huge Taiwanese flag pinned to the wall, scribbled with the climbers' names from a particular Taiwanese expedition. Mel has a big grin on his face as he reads it. He points out some additional Chinese characters scrawled across the middle.

'See that,' he says. 'They are not from Taiwan expedition. It says "Taiwan belongs to China".'

I'm too polite to ask whether he too believes Taiwan belongs to China, but judging by his reaction I suspect that he doesn't give a toss, any more than I would care if someone scrawled 'Las Malvinas belong to Argentina' across a poster of a lonely sheep in a windswept field on the Falkland Islands.

It takes another thirty minutes to reach Base Camp, and it's an exhilarating experience for me. I have read about this place so many times and carried a mental picture of it in my mind. Now I am seeing it for real. I recognise many of the peaks from photos. Pumori, Lingtren, Khumbutse, Changtse, the West Shoulder and Nuptse enclose this natural amphitheatre.

At first, I find it hard to piece things together. The Khumbu Icefall, our route into the Western Cwm, is hidden from view during the approach. It's a secret opening onto Everest's upper reaches from the south side, but until you realise it's there, Everest appears to be guarded by impossible faces. For a long time I look at the towering glaciers and cliffs of the Lho La, believing it to be the Khumbu Icefall. This wall of rock and ice, which forms a pass into Tibet, looks nothing like the obstacle I imagined.

There are sections of rock leading me to speculate that there hasn't been much snowfall this year. This feeling is reinforced when Everest's black pyramid appears above the West Shoulder. It's as bare of snow as it looked when we climbed it from the north side two years ago. Then gradually the opening appears to the right of the valley, and the Icefall spills out.

When they first explored Everest from the south side in 1950, Bill Tilman and Charles Houston must have had a similar experience. They would have needed to walk almost to the top of the valley before they spotted this route up into the Western Cwm. Only then would they have realised Everest might just be climbable from Nepal.

It's a picturesque approach along a ridge of moraine. At 11.30 we drop down and cross a jumble of boulders to the maze of tents that is Base Camp. Tents of all shapes and sizes sprawl across the moraine like a shanty town. We see Phil waiting for us above the Altitude Junkies' encampment. When he ushers us into the plush, carpeted dining tent, which I recognise from previous expeditions, it feels like I am coming home. Those of the team who have never been on a Junkies expedition are impressed.

The approach to Everest Base Camp. The tents of Base Camp can be seen front left. Changtse is the rock peak back left. The Lho La is the pass in front of it. The main triangular peak in the photo is Everest's West Shoulder. The black summit of Everest can be seen peeping up behind the West Shoulder. The peak on the right is a shoulder of Nuptse. The Khumbu Icefall spills down the gap between the West Shoulder and Nuptse.

When we are all assembled for lunch I decide to try a little mischief.

'Mel graffitied "Taiwan belongs to China" on a Taiwanese flag at the teahouse in Gorak Shep,' I say.

Mel looks horrified. 'No, no,' he says. 'I not write it myself, I just said someone else write it.'

I feel embarrassed. He's so upset that we might suspect him of such a mischievous deed that I end up having to apologise.

Our first happy hour of the expedition begins at four o'clock. Our chef Da Pasang serves red wine, cheese, Pringles and sushi in the dining tent. Ian leads the way. Every so often he gathers up the glasses to replenish them from the kitchen tent. The wine is very good. I'm already feeling light-headed after the first one, but Ian makes me drink three more.

Conversation inevitably turns to Everest, and we talk about Tilman and Houston's Everest reconnaissance. The great British mountain explorer Bill Tilman made the first ever exploration of the southern approach to Everest in 1950 with American mountaineer Charles Houston. They had only two days to explore a possible route. On the first day they headed towards the Lho La. George Mallory had already looked down from here into the Khumbu Icefall and Western Cwm when he explored the Tibetan side in 1921. Tilman knew there were two keys to climbing Everest from the south. They needed to find a practical route from the top of the Western Cwm to the South Col, and there must be a route up the ridge from the South Col to Everest's summit.

Their first exploration proved unsuccessful. As they walked towards the Lho La, a 'trick of lighting' (as Tilman described it) prevented them even seeing a route into the Western Cwm. Trick of lighting, my arse. As I noticed myself earlier today, the Khumbu Icefall spills down from a narrow gap. Tilman and Houston were a mile short of the foot of the Lho La when they turned around. The Icefall was still concealed, as it had been for me, initially. They spotted it easily the following day. On the second day they decided to climb Kala Pattar, the well-known viewpoint above Gorak Shep. Here they discovered what many trekkers know: a shoulder of Nuptse obscures the South Col from Kala Pattar. With the South Col hidden, there was no way of knowing whether there was a possible route up from the Western Cwm.

The second question, about a route from the South Col to the summit, also proved elusive. From Kala Pattar they thought the south ridge of Everest looked a bit too steep, but Tilman deduced correctly that he wasn't looking at the ridge, but a buttress protruding from the South-West Face. In fact, Everest's southern approach is not a south ridge, but a south-east one which is not as steep as the angle looks from Kala Pattar. Tilman's friend Eric Shipton answered some of these questions the following year.

Phil is pleased to see us. He said the Sherpas made him eat on his own in the dining tent last night instead of letting him eat with them. He seems upset by this.

'But what's the problem with that, Phil?' Louis says. 'If you ate on your own then it means you were with all your friends.'

DAY 10
SETTLING IN AT BASE CAMP

Saturday 12th of April, 2014 – Everest Base Camp, Nepal

My health seems to be deteriorating. I didn't get much sleep last night, and this morning I have a headache, a cold, and a bad cough. Not surprisingly, I'm still tired.

There are a couple of nice day hikes from Base Camp for elevated views of Everest and Lhotse. Both summits are invisible from Base Camp, hidden behind Nuptse and Everest's West Shoulder, but you only need to trek a short distance up Pumori, the mountain opposite, to see right into the Western Cwm.

It's only a short hike up to Camp 1 on Pumori. Or if we prefer, we can trek back to Gorak Shep and walk up to the famous viewpoint of Kala Pattar, a shoulder of the same mountain. But until I've got over this illness I'll be staying in camp and resting. I hope I'll be able to shake it off in a couple of days.

It's a cold morning, with little sun to recharge the solar panels. There is much talk of technology. We have two main methods of communicating with the outside world. The first is the Nepalese NCell phone network, meant to provide 3G connectivity for those members of the team who bought NCell SIM cards when they were in Kathmandu. The second is the BGAN/Inmarsat satellite system.

The leader of another team tells Phil that both systems were working well until a couple of days ago. Then Asian Trekking, a Nepalese trekking agency, pitched up with giant satellite dishes. Now the 3G and BGAN no longer work, but there is a third option: Asian Trekking are selling internet packages at $7,000 USD for the season. I try not to make a connection between these events.

I have a lazy morning reading, shaving and sleeping. At one point we are summoned outside to meet our thirty-strong Sherpa team. I know many of them already from previous expeditions, but our team is much bigger this year. Half of our Sherpas are new to me. The new guys have worked regularly for the American operator Mountain Trip, but Mountain Trip do not have a team on Everest this year, and they are very happy to be taken into the Junkies' fold for a season.

We all stand in a big circle beside the stone platform that is being erected for tomorrow's puja. One by one Dorje introduces the Sherpas by name. Then it comes to us, and we each have to introduce ourselves.

'I'm Mark from England. This is my fourth time with the Junkies. I have twice summited with Chongba,' I say, pointing towards him as he grins back, 'on Everest north side and Manaslu.'

After lunch Phil demonstrates the new Summit Oxygen apparatus we will be using on the summit push. This is a new brand that hasn't been available before. The old system that I used on Manaslu and Everest had several drawbacks. The regulator gave inaccurate readings – I wasn't sure how much oxygen I was breathing. It had a bottle-shaped oxygen reservoir that swung around my chest as I walked, and got in the way. One of its valves, for taking in ambient air, was always icing up. The outlet valve dripped water onto the zipper of my down suit, freezing it closed.

Most annoying of all was the rubber mask that came with it, which often formed a suction gag against my face. This might have gone down well at Ann Summers parties, but on the North Ridge of Everest – where you need every gram of oxygen you can get – it was less than convenient.

Phil says the new system doesn't suffer from these deficiencies. I have a love-hate relationship with oxygen apparatus. When it works it's great, but often I've felt I wasn't getting much benefit from it. It's been too unreliable, and I'm hoping this new kit will be better.

At dinner this evening we have a discussion about Mallory and Irvine, who disappeared on Everest in 1924. Nobody knows whether they reached the summit, and we speculate about what happened to them. A research team found Mallory's body high on the North Face in 1999, and his injuries suggested he had died in a fall. The researchers had hoped to find a camera on the body, which could have confirmed whether the pair reached the top, but they were disappointed. Irvine's body has never been found, and many Everest historians believe he must have been carrying the camera instead of Mallory.

But Phil believes that the Chinese team who climbed Everest in 1960 did find Irvine's body. He thinks they kept his camera to hide the evidence. The Chinese ascent in 1960 is now regarded as the first ascent of Everest from the north side, but Phil thinks they didn't get there. I tell him I think he has bought a conspiracy theory. I have read their account of the ascent. It's a bit weird, with lots of Communist propaganda, but their description of the summit route is plausible.

Phil also believes he may have seen Irvine's body during one of his many climbs of Everest from the north.

'There was a piece of tweed on my right as I came down from the Exit Cracks,' he says. The Exit Cracks are a series of rocky slabs at a point where the route leaves the North-East Ridge and diverts down the North Face.

There is a chance Irvine's body is lying on the North Face in roughly that location. But Phil's sighting also tallies with the position of the 1933 Everest team's high camp. Eric Shipton and Frank Smythe made their summit attempt from there, and Smythe described seeing a UFO on the way down (I suspect he was using faulty oxygen apparatus, powered by some local herb). It's more likely Phil saw the remains of their camp instead of Sandy Irvine's body.

Later in the evening a lama (monk) arrives from Pangboche. He has come to conduct our puja in the morning, and after dinner Dorje tells Phil he has agreed to let the lama sleep in the communications tent.

We are still without 3G or satellite connectivity.

'Can he bless the BGAN while he's in there,' we ask.

DAY 11
THE PUJA

Sunday 13th of April, 2014 – Everest Base Camp, Nepal

Peter, a 61-year-old lawyer, arrives at breakfast this morning and sits down with a puzzled look on his face.

'Has anyone else been experiencing strange dreams?' he asks.

Many people have vivid dreams at high altitude when they are still acclimatising. There are various theories why this happens, but the most likely reason is broken sleep. You keep waking up, and dreams remain fresh in your mind.

There are a few nods around the table as we wait for Peter to continue.

'I dreamt that I was driving along the freeway when a police officer pulled alongside and signalled for me to pull over. The cop came to the window and asked for my licence, and whether I'd been drinking. I looked up and saw Phil Crampton in a policeman's uniform. "No need to take me to the station, officer," I replied. "I'm guilty as hell."'

'Don't tell me,' Jay says. 'Then a red light started flashing, and Phil began singing "YMCA"?'

Peter shakes his head. 'Nothing like that. Or if there was, I woke up while Phil still had his clothes on.'

Our puja begins straight after breakfast. It's a beautiful morning, and our Sherpas have erected a puja platform beneath a hillside of moraine. The setting is dramatic for a monk to chant prayers, looking across the glacier to Nuptse. The lama from Pangboche has one of our kitchen crew, Phu Dorje, as his assistant. We are told Phu Dorje once trained as a monk in an earlier life.

These ceremonies to appease the mountain gods before a climb can last for a long time. This morning the lama keeps it relatively short, and chants for perhaps an hour before asking our Sherpas to erect the prayer flags. They raise a flagpole above the puja platform and string rows of flags from the pole like bunting, extending to the four corners of camp.

Raising the prayer flags, with the West Shoulder behind

We stand up and throw rice into the air. We're supposed to throw it three times, an auspicious number, but I lose count of the number of tosses and just keep following the lama.

Then we line up for a blessing, taking it in turns to kneel in front of him. He ties necklaces with mini books of prayers around our necks, which we are meant to keep on for the rest of the expedition, even when we sleep.

Then the ceremony is over and the lama moves on to his next appointment with another team. For our Sherpas this is a signal for the drinking to start. It's not even ten o'clock, and a Tuborg beer is thrust into my hand.

Tarke lurks with a bottle of Khukri Rum, urging each of us to down shots, which he pours into the cap. We have to take them in threes because (guess what), three is an auspicious number. Pasang Nima hovers with a big kettle of chang and a clutch of tin mugs. This is a local rice beer that resembles milk, but is rather more potent. He is a small man, but immensely powerful on the mountain, and we call him the Pocket Rocket. This morning he reveals a different quality – an elfin ability to appear from nowhere as soon as my mug is empty, and refill it before I have time to protest. I spend much of the morning trying to hide behind a rock whenever I see him, but usually he spots me. A few times my chang 'accidentally' finds its way onto the ground, but I soon realise this is a futile manoeuvre. The Pocket Rocket is always quick to notice, and eventually I discover the only way to avoid his chang is to hold a cup full to the brim at all times.

In the middle of this mayhem Robert appears with his trekking friend Scott. They have just completed their trek into the Gokyo Valley and crossed the Cho La pass. They may have been expecting a low-key welcome when they reached Base Camp, but as soon as we realise they are here, we begin whooping and cheering.

Robert is a teetotaller and Scott is only here for the trek. Technically Scott isn't required to appease the mountain gods by drinking, but he doesn't know this. Ian convinces him that Robert needs a proxy to drink on his behalf or the gods will be angry. Scott is a good-natured character, and finds himself unable to refuse.

'I can't remember the last time I was drunk before noon,' Peter says to me during a quiet moment.

When I was on the north side of Everest in 2012, our puja lasted all day, but this time it fizzles out at lunchtime. In the afternoon I retire to my tent for some sleep, but the Sherpas continue their celebrations.

Later in the afternoon Phil is summoned to resolve a dispute. They are due to do a load carry into the Khumbu Icefall tomorrow. One of them, Ang Gelu, refuses to join in because Margaret has hired him as her personal Sherpa. He believes this should exempt him from carrying some of the group equipment.

But there are several personal Sherpas on the team this year. Among the Lhotse climbers, Margaret is the only one who has hired a personal Sherpa. Ang Gelu will climb with her at all times, but the rest of us will only climb with a Sherpa on summit day. Most of the time we will be climbing on our own.

The Everest team have paid for a different level of service. They have all been assigned a personal Sherpa, and will even have a second Sherpa climbing with them on summit day too.

Cynics will say they need a second Sherpa to carry them up, but this is disingenuous. Nobody gets carried up Everest, and statements like this betray a lack of understanding. Whatever the level of support, you've got to get up on your own two feet. It's safer for Sherpas to climb two to a client. If anything should go wrong in that extreme environment, there are more resources to call upon. Of course, it also helps the Sherpa community, as it means more jobs for them.

But in truth I believe this is more than any competent climber needs. Two personal Sherpas on summit day is a new thing. It is one of the many 'luxuries' pushing the price of Everest expeditions up to unaffordable levels.

Ang Gelu's stance is not popular with the other Sherpas who have been assigned to members of the Everest team. They will be doing their share of load carrying too. Phil takes their side and threatens to fine Ang Gelu unless he toes the line.

This upsets Margaret. She believes Ang Gelu should be treated as a special case because she is paying extra for him. If she paid extra, why should we be making use of him when we did not pay?

I can see her point as far as the other Lhotse climbers are concerned. We have paid a mere $20,000 to be here, but the Everest climbers have paid a whopping $45,000 – far more than any of us, Margaret included.

But there are other considerations too. It's fine for some people to pay more for a better level of service, as long as it doesn't affect the service of those who have paid less. If Ang Gelu has angered the other Sherpas, who perceive him to be getting away with doing less work, then they in turn may wonder why they work so hard.

I may not have paid as much as the others, but I have still paid an awful lot of money. I want to climb with a happy Chongba on summit day, not an aggrieved Chongba.

Ultimately, we are a team. Some people can dig deeper into their pockets, and they expect more from the team because they paid more money for their expedition. But the well-being of the team as a whole matters more; this should take priority and shape decisions.

But of course, I don't have to carry a huge load up the mountain like Ang Gelu, so I guess I would say that.

We have to trust Phil and Dorje to make decisions about

Sherpa dynamics. One of the reasons we climb with Altitude Junkies is because they have a great Sherpa crew.

I am sorry to hear Ang Gelu has been the cause of tension, because I like him. I had a good chat with him at the puja. Two years ago he helped my friend Mark Dickson, who is prone to frostbite, to reach the summit of Everest. Ang Gelu clipped and unclipped Mark from every anchor so that he didn't have to remove his gloves. When I was struggling to climb a difficult section of the Second Step, it was Ang Gelu who climbed above me and proffered a hand to help me up. So I too have him to thank for my summit success. It's something I won't forget.

DAY 12
LADDER TRAINING

Monday 14th of April, 2014 – Everest Base Camp, Nepal

I have another good night's sleep and feel like I'm starting to get over my little illness. As I get ready for eight o'clock breakfast I go for a pee, and see Phil, Dorje and Ang Gelu fixing two ladders over a stream below camp. They are making preparations for a ladder training session after breakfast. Ang Gelu was meant to be carrying a fifteen-kilogram load up the Khumbu Icefall this morning. I conclude that Margaret must have won her argument with Phil.

You may wonder why such a training session is necessary. Any fool can climb a ladder, after all. But speed is of the essence when moving through the treacherous terrain of the Khumbu Icefall. It's not so easy to climb a series of ladders strapped together, that flex beneath you as you stare into a yawning crevasse. Crampons don't make it any easier. There are ropes on either side to act as handrails, and there's a certain technique to keeping them taut as you cross. You have to clip in and out of them at each anchor point. Climbers who have not mastered these techniques keep everyone waiting as they edge across nervously, or fumble with their carabiner as they clip in and out of the rope. With towers of ice that threaten to collapse, snow bridges in danger of melting, and regular avalanches from the mountains on either side, the Khumbu Icefall is not a place to linger for too long.

After breakfast we unpack our boots, crampons and harness/jumar rigs, and go onto the ice. The training is straightforward. We cross a pair of horizontal ladders, climb a pair of vertical ladders tied together, then traverse back down again. I haven't had much practice crossing ladders while wearing crampons, so it's a good confidence booster for me.

Ladder practice on the Khumbu Glacier

Ricardo seems as healthy as the rest of us, but after lunch he tells us he needs to have his blood pressure checked at the Himalayan Rescue Association (HRA) medical facility at the other end of camp. The HRA is a charity founded in the 1970s with the aim of reducing illness in the mountains of Nepal. Since 2003 it has maintained a temporary health clinic at Everest Base Camp during the climbing season, staffed entirely by volunteer doctors and nurses. It's known affectionately as Everest ER, and we've all paid a contribution this year to make use of its services should we need them.

Ricardo seems to be popular with the ladies (as most musicians are), and has therefore acquired the reputation as the team Casanova. When he announces that he'll be visiting the hospital, it's the signal for more ribald humour.

'Are you sure you're ill, Ricardo, or are you just going to check the nurses out?'

'If you're looking to raise your blood pressure, you can save yourself a walk. Robert has some Viagra.'

It snows for most of the afternoon. The sky remains overcast, but just before dinner the clouds lift, providing our mountain amphitheatre with a vast open roof. This makes for a bitterly cold evening, but it also gives us a few moments to contemplate the panorama all around us. The sun touches Changtse on the Tibetan side of the Lho La, bathing the rocks in an orange glow. Then it falls from the sky and plunges us into darkness.

DAY 13
A WALK TO PUMORI BASE CAMP

Tuesday 15th of April, 2014 – Everest Base Camp, Nepal

I've had a few days of rest now, so today I decide to make my first journey out of Base Camp since arriving here. It's a clear morning, and after breakfast I set out with Louis, Ian, Kevin and Caroline to trek up to Pumori Base Camp. Somewhere a couple of hundred metres above Everest Base Camp, I've been told there is a viewpoint where we can gaze right into the Western Cwm.

We begin by following the trail back to Gorak Shep until we reach the moraine ridge. Robert, who has been to Pumori Base Camp, told me to look for a path on the right at this point, underneath a giant boulder. I see nothing obvious, and end up guessing the route. I turn out to be wrong. Almost immediately we find ourselves scrambling up a steep bank of scree. By the time we reach the top we are all exhausted and have to stop for a few deep breaths.

Still we can see no obvious path, though there are several small cairns that lead us across boulder fields. Like Robert, Louis has been to Pumori Base Camp before, but he doesn't seem to be any clearer about the route than I am.

We wander around for ten to fifteen minutes until we see an Adventure Consultants group – another expedition operator – amble past some distance to our right. They are being led by one of their Sherpas, who clearly knows the way.

We follow behind them for a while, and when they stop, Kevin and then Louis are able to take up the trail. There is some boulder-hopping, but also places where the terrain is firmer. After an hour and a half we reach a large bench-like rock on a flatter area of moraine matted with grass. Here Louis stops.

'We are at Pumori Base Camp,' he says.

I look back, and let out a whistle. Although we can't quite see right into the Western Cwm as promised, it doesn't matter. This is the closest I have come to the classic, picture-postcard view of Everest above the Khumbu Icefall, and I have to pinch myself.

Everest peeps up behind the West Shoulder as the tangled mass of crumbling ice that is the Khumbu Icefall spills into the valley beneath us. Lhotse appears distant at its top end, a strange mix of ice and black rock the shape of a cowboy hat. It stands at the end of the corridor, and attracts my fascination in a different way to Everest, which towers over it to the left. Lhotse is the peak we hope to climb, after all.

I've seen a similar view many times in photographs, but this is the first time I've looked at it for real. Louis is the only one of us to have climbed Everest from the south, so he explains the route up, and the position of camps on the Lhotse Face. It looks horribly steep, but we are viewing it head on, which always makes it look worse than it is.

To the left we can see Everest's North Col, where we camped two years ago. The North Ridge, our old route of ascent, is still hidden behind the West Shoulder. The vast North Face slants away from us, appearing as just a narrow sliver of rock from this angle. We stay for about fifteen minutes contemplating this spacious amphitheatre of mountains, but it's a little chilly, so at eleven o'clock we head down again.

Admiring Everest, Lhotse and Nuptse from Pumori Base Camp

Just before we rejoin the main trail we meet Margaret and Edita on their way up. They delayed their departure to assist with the evacuation of a Chinese climber. The sky has been alive with helicopters this morning. A surprising number of climbers are being evacuated after reaching Base Camp too quickly and ending up with altitude sickness.

As we look out over this tented village between steep mountain walls, Margaret makes a casual remark.

'There are less than half as many tents as there were in 2011, when I was last here.'

This becomes the subject of discussion when we return to Base Camp for lunch. We already talked about the situation with Lukla flights when we were in Namche with

Siling. The shortage of flights may have reduced the number of trekkers in the Khumbu region, but Everest climbers are different. If you are paying thousands of dollars for your expedition, the flights become a minor problem which you find a solution for, even if it means paying a little more. Flights aren't the reason there are fewer climbers here this year.

Phil believes last year's fight between Sherpas and western climbers, and the media storm that accompanied it, has put many people off. I believe the drip feed of absurd announcements by the Nepalese government has also had an adverse effect.

These silly announcements have included stationing police and army at Base Camp to keep the peace between Sherpas and westerners. This provision is supposed to be put in place this year, but we are all sceptical whether it will actually happen. It includes putting a liaison officer at Base Camp to 'constrain bizarre records' and ensure none of us engage in any madcap stunts. The liaison officer will have a challenging time of it this year. The Discovery Channel have already announced they will be sending a large film crew to Base Camp to make a documentary about the extreme sportsman Joby Ogwyn. Ogwyn intends to climb to the summit and jump off in a wingsuit, like a flying squirrel.

We have been told that helicopter flights will be restricted to medical emergencies only, and that we each have to carry eight kilograms of trash down from the high camps. There has been talk of installing a ladder on the Hillary Step to make it easier for everyone (or 'ease congestion').

Each announcement created its own shower of media vitriol, tarnishing Everest in the eyes of potential visitors. But Robert believes they won't have had much impact.

'Maybe you're right, but I'm not so sure. These

announcements were all pretty recent. People plan their Everest climb years ahead.'

It's a good point. Robert is a wise man, and I respect his opinion on many things.

At least, I do until lunchtime.

As we are finishing our dessert we find ourselves having a strange conversation about guns. I say strange, but in America I guess these conversations are normal. Robert and Peter – two highly intelligent people, both of whom own a great many guns – explain to us the details of the Second Amendment and right to bear arms. Their explanation is a little esoteric, and those of us from countries where guns are difficult to get hold of find it quite baffling. We grill them enthusiastically.

Peter and Robert smile at us benignly, like primary school teachers patiently explaining the 'ou' vowel sound to a small child. They remain silent while we amuse ourselves. We come from different cultures, and there's a gulf in understanding that we're not going to bridge before the end of the cheesecake (which was delicious). Fortunately, despite their penchant for firearms, Robert and Peter are good-natured people. They take no offence at our jokes, and the conversation moves on.

DAY 14
ICEFALL FEARS

Wednesday 16th of April, 2014 – Everest Base Camp, Nepal

I decide to make today another lazy one. Last night, Ian and Louis agreed to go up to Kala Pattar today for another acclimatisation hike. It's quite some distance above Gorak Shep, which means they leave before breakfast. I decline their invitation to accompany them.

There's a bit of a breeze at Base Camp and I think it may be windy higher up. I spend the morning doing some laundry, and as the clouds swirl past the peaks around us I'm glad of my decision.

At breakfast Phil updates us on the 3G and general comms situation.

'My wife Trish spoke to the head honcho at NCell last night. He said he didn't know we couldn't get 3G at Base Camp, but that he would look into it.'

Without 3G I still have no means of blogging. I am starting to accept it will remain the case until I return to Kathmandu after the expedition.

As I sit outside my tent this morning with a bowl of water, I talk to Edita. She is preparing to go for a walk up to Pumori Base Camp with Margaret.

'You could see if you can get 3G up there,' I say to her.

During the trek from Lukla she was more active than

any of us in searching for an internet connection.

'You know what, I've given up worrying about 3G or NCell,' she says. 'And now it feels like I have more freedom.'

I find myself nodding in agreement. We are here to climb a mountain and enjoy the Himalayas. Worrying about posting messages in order to update people back home is a distraction that mars the experience.

Only half of the team are in camp at one o'clock, when lunch is due to be served. Phil instructs Da Pasang to bring it anyway. While we are eating he leaves the dining tent to take a phone call. He returns with a big grin on his face.

'That was the head honcho at NCell,' he says. 'It looks like we're going to get 3G after all. He called to apologise that it wasn't available. He said he's looking into it.'

I don't know precisely what role a 'head honcho' has, but it's hard to believe it's anyone too senior. NCell is a major national telecoms company, responsible for all the mobile cellular towers in the Khumbu and elsewhere in Nepal. It seems unlikely that the head of the company would phone Phil – who provides only a tiny fraction of their custom – to apologise personally.

I'm not surprised when we don't see Ian and Louis for lunch. Ian was keen for me to join them on the walk to Kala Pattar because he said that I 'set a good pace'. I don't think he meant walking.

When we climbed Manaslu together three years ago, Ian made regular visits down to the village of Samagaon for beers in the teahouse. With Gorak Shep and its teahouses conveniently located on the way back from Kala Pattar, I have little doubt what has delayed them. With great confidence I tell everyone that we can expect them back for four o'clock happy hour.

I'm surprised when I see them appear on the slopes above camp at two o'clock, but when Robert appears behind them I understand why. They had a responsible adult looking after them.

Later there is some concerning news. For several days our Sherpas have been complaining about the Icefall Doctors – the Sherpa team contracted by the Sagarmatha Pollution Control Committee (SPCC) to fix the route through the Khumbu Icefall. Our Sherpas are saying that the Icefall Doctors have not done a very good job, and there are places where the ladders are dangerous.

Phil has learned that a Sherpa from Russell Brice's Himex team fell off a ladder today. Although he wasn't badly hurt, it's more than just a bad omen. Phil and Dorje talk about accompanying our Sherpa team on their carry through the Icefall tonight, to assess the safety of the route for themselves.

Until now only Sherpas have been through it. It will be a different matter when clients have to follow. They are much slower and often considerably less experienced. Ice towers can collapse at any time, crevasses can open up, and avalanches can tumble from the mountains on either side. It's not a place to linger, or bugger around trying to get up a precarious ladder as people wait behind you.

DAY 15
THE ICEFALL

Thursday 17th of April, 2014 – Everest Base Camp, Nepal

Phil is still here at breakfast this morning. He didn't join the Sherpas on their latest carry to Camp 2, to assess the route, but he now has an alternative plan for the Icefall. He suggests we all make a short one- to two-hour foray up into the ice tomorrow to keep us from going stir crazy.

There's some logic to this. It sounds like the route will not be ready for a few days, and we've been here at Base Camp for several days now without much action. Lethargy is settling in. If we can't go higher yet, then a brief spell in the Icefall will help to keep us interested.

It's cold and windy after breakfast. Instead of joining some of the others for another walk down to Gorak Shep, I decide to go up the valley for my first look at the rest of Everest Base Camp. Our tents are at the bottom end. Since we arrived I've been no higher, and I'm keen to get a better sense of what Base Camp is like.

Our camp – and those of our neighbours, Himex and International Mountain Guides (IMG) – turns out to be in an outlying village. I pass through a grey belt of glacier before reaching the rest of camp.

Base Camp is long and sprawling. It takes me about forty minutes to walk from one end to the other at my slow, ambling pace. I discover that it's far from being the shanty town of tents often portrayed. Everywhere I look tents nestle in folds of moraine or perch on ridges, but there is plenty of space for everyone. The area could easily accommodate twice as many tents without difficulty.

Eventually I reach the camp of a big Indian team at the far end, and find myself staring right up the Icefall between the West Shoulder and Nuptse. I see figures coming down between walls of seracs. It doesn't look quite so intimidating from here.

For many years I have dreamed about this place. The Khumbu Icefall is one of Everest's most famous (and infamous) features. I've been to the summit from the north side, but this is the first time I've looked up the crumpled heap of broken ice that stretches into the far distance.

The immensity of this ice sheet, hundreds of metres thick, is difficult to comprehend. Within its folds are crevasses so vast they would swallow an ocean liner many times over. Some of these chasms are hidden by tiny cracks that entirely disappear under newly fallen snow. Rising above them are towers of leaning ice that would dwarf many skyscrapers, ready to topple with a slight movement of the glacier or warming of the sun, and there is no hope of survival if you are passing underneath. A party of climbers roped together would be crushed as easily as ants beneath a hobnailed boot.

I'm well aware of its fearsome reputation, and the people who have lost their lives within its towering corridors. The first was Jake Breitenbach, a young American climber who was forging a route through the Icefall in 1963. A large section of ice collapsed with a roar. He was roped to two other climbers, who survived the accident with the help of teammates who came to their aid. The rescuers could see no trace of Breitenbach. The rope led down into many tons of giant ice blocks. He must have been killed instantly.

In the last fifty years there have been thirty more deaths here, either from collapsing ice, avalanches or falls into crevasses. The overwhelming majority of victims have been Sherpas, who spend so much more time exposed to danger as they carry heavy loads up and down the mountain.

I'm aware of all these things, but I also know there are few places like it anywhere. It can only be seen to be believed. I'm relishing the opportunity to explore further, and looking forward to our little foray tomorrow.

A majestic-looking Khumbu Icefall from Everest Base Camp

DAY 16
TRAGEDY

Friday 18th of April, 2014 – Everest Base Camp, Nepal

I blink awake at 5.15. It's light, with only a whisper of wind on the tent, and surprisingly mild. I was expecting to get dressed with freezing fingers, but this isn't too bad. There is little to indicate that today will be unusual.

We have breakfast at six o'clock. All twelve clients on our team are up to make our first short foray into the Khumbu Icefall. Phil, Dorje and Ang Gelu are with us, but our other Sherpas are all having a lie-in. They have earned a good rest after carrying more of our equipment up to Camp 2 yesterday.

Before a climb, I don't find it easy to eat this early in the morning. I force down a few mouthfuls of toast and push my egg and beans to one side. We leave one by one from 6.30 as we each complete our preparations for departure. I leave on my own and walk through Base Camp to the edge of the glacier, repeating yesterday's footsteps.

I walk for about fifteen minutes, absorbed in my thoughts. Getting up and ready is always the hardest part. Once I am moving, any nerves are gone, and I relax into my stride, focusing on my steps.

'Hey, Mark, have you seen that? Look up there!' I hear Jay cry out behind me.

Avalanches are common in high mountain environments. They fall throughout the day in inaccessible locations, presenting little danger. If their rumble, similar to the noise of thunder, lasts longer than usual, I sometimes look up to watch, but mostly I ignore them. I rarely reach for my camera to film, like some people do. Usually the moment has passed by the time I am ready, and it's not worth the effort.

On this occasion I didn't even notice another one falling at first, and had it not been for Jay I might even have missed it.

But no; I soon realise I could not have missed this one.

I look up into the Khumbu Icefall. An enormous veil of white dust, one of the biggest avalanches I have ever seen, has engulfed the entire breadth from the West Shoulder to Nuptse. It surges like a tsunami on the skyline, at the point where the Icefall disappears into the Western Cwm. It's so big that we both have plenty of time to reach for our cameras. Jay takes some video footage, and I manage to snap a still shot. Time seems to stand still. It's a while before the cloud disperses into cracks in the glacier and all is silent again.

A few thoughts pass through my mind. First there is incredulity. 'Are we really about to go up into that thing?' I think to myself.

But a moment later a sense of relief washes over me. 'Thank heavens our Sherpas aren't up there now.'

This feeling intensifies when I think how late we set off this morning. Yesterday we discussed the possibility of leaving at three o'clock to give us a chance to climb while the ice was hard. None of us relished getting up so early when we were only thinking of doing a short walk, and after some thought we rejected the plan. I feel a sharp sensation in the pit of my stomach. Had we done so, then there is every chance we would have been right up there at the critical moment. That cloud would have swallowed us.

Over the years I've heard many eyewitness accounts from people who have been in the Icefall when an avalanche fell. They all described a moment of panic when they heard it crashing down, but didn't know where it was coming from. They had just enough time to duck behind the most sheltered ice tower they could find, where they spent a few nervous moments wondering what fate had in store for them. They felt a woof of air, then a light – or sometimes heavy – dusting of snow. Finally there was relief. They survived to tell the story, after all.

The moment when a gigantic avalanche engulfs the entire breadth of the Khumbu Icefall

Avalanches in the Icefall don't have to be fatal; it's possible to survive them. But this one was so enormous it hardly seems possible…

I don't know for how long these thoughts pass through

my mind. Rarely in my life have I had to face tragedy. My first instinct is to assume things will be OK, however unlikely that may seem. But I soon realise that there are sure to be Sherpas from other teams up there.

Jay has been into the Icefall before, when he attempted Everest a few years ago. For the next few minutes we swap stories of risk and danger, refusing to accept what we've just seen.

Up ahead of us, Ian, Robert, Kevin and Louis were walking together when they heard a loud crack. They looked up in time to see a huge section of ice collapse from the West Shoulder. It crashed onto the northern edge of the valley floor, triggering the tidal wave of snow that we watched sweep all the way across to the other side.

We catch up with them at the bottom of the glacier.

'Did you see that avalanche?' I ask.

'Hell, yeah,' Robert says. 'Man, that's bad news. There's people up there.'

It's not until Dorje arrives that I realise the scale of the horror that's about to unfold – that is unfolding as we stand there, looking up into the ice.

'How many Sherpa?' I ask him, pointing up the Icefall.

'Maybe forty, fifty,' he replies. His expression is serious, yet otherwise inscrutable.

He is a veteran of these mountains, and he must have understood the consequences much quicker than I did. Was he shocked by what he saw, or is he too familiar with mountaineering accidents by now? I don't think about these things, because the figure he has uttered – an underestimate, as it turns out – causes my jaw to drop.

Forty or fifty Sherpas?

We can only hope most were above or below when the avalanche swept across. Perhaps they had time to take shelter behind seracs, but I realise this is a forlorn hope. Such a huge quantity of snow came down that it's hard to believe anyone caught underneath isn't buried there still.

Dorje and Ang Gelu head up the Icefall almost immediately. It's a natural reaction. Both are likely to have close friends somewhere up there.

Phil radios back to camp to try and rouse more of our Sherpas to come and help. They are having a well-earned rest after their load carry into the Icefall yesterday. But four of them – Pasang Ongchu, Kami, Kusang and Samden – put on their climbing gear and arrive only minutes later.

Phil goes into the Icefall with them, but the rest of us can only watch – our foray is over, and now we are helpless bystanders. We are not acclimatised. It would take us many hours to get to the avalanche site, and we would only get in the way of any rescue, wheezing up a narrow trail when others need to move quickly along it. It would be like crawling under the feet of firefighters as they rush into a burning building.

For the next two hours we stand on a little ridge at the foot of the Icefall, watching events unfold above us. Through the zoom lenses of our cameras we can see dozens of tiny dots emerging from the ice. Many figures cluster in a single location on the skyline, close to where the avalanche sped across. We can see smaller clumps of people lower down, descending to camp. All are moving and, as Dorje said, there could easily be forty or fifty of them. It seems a miracle so many have survived.

A cameraman appears on the ice ridge, part of a team from the Discovery Channel. They are here to film the extreme athlete Joby Ogwyn, who intends to climb to the summit of Everest and jump off in a wing suit.

The cameraman asks Edita to explain to camera what she saw this morning. She doesn't want to, and points him towards me. I have mixed feelings, because I know what a media circus is likely to result from this event, especially if there are fatalities. I agree to do it, but I'm quite shell-shocked, and not very coherent. I hope those few seconds end up on the cutting-room floor.[1]

The cameraman brings bad news. He tells us that four Sherpas from their team, Alpine Ascents, are not responding to radio calls. Radios are crackling behind us in Base Camp. We learn that another Sherpa is critically injured.

One by one we end our vigil and wander back to camp. I leave at nine o'clock, more than two hours after the avalanche.

The place is busy now. Many people are gathering round the helipads, though the sky is still silent. I wonder why it's taking them so long. A single helicopter buzzed into the Icefall only a few minutes after the avalanche. I guessed they were assessing the situation, but there have been no choppers since.

Back at our camp I pack away my climbing gear, get changed, then join the rest of our team. They are all together, clients and Sherpas, watching events unfold from outside the kitchen tent.

The first helicopters arrive at ten o'clock. To begin with they make some reconnaissance runs, but after a while they land in the Icefall and pick up casualties. Most of the casualties are brought down to the Himalayan Rescue Association medical facility here in Base Camp. One is flown straight out to Lukla.

Then we watch in shock as a helicopter emerges from the Icefall with a longline swinging beneath it. A figure hangs by its torso at the end of the rope, its face to the sky and four limbs dangling below.

'I don't like the look of this one,' I say while it is still some way off. 'This looks like a body.'

Hundreds of onlookers watch in horror as the helicopter hovers above Base Camp with its macabre burden. Then, at the last moment, the figure tilts onto its feet as the chopper comes into land.

'I think he's alive,' Kevin says, and we breathe a collective sigh of relief.

It's one of the only moments of hope. For the next hour we watch in disbelief as a single helicopter makes journey after journey into the Icefall. One by one, bodies are brought down on a longline. We lose count of how many. It's relentless. Crowds gather at the helipads. The living are taken to the medical tent, but many are corpses. Every once in a while the helicopter stops to refuel before rising into the Icefall once again.

Another casualty is lowered into Base Camp on a longline

Our Sherpas are listening to the radios. They are better informed than we are about what's going on. Most of the people helping up in the Icefall are Sherpas, and most of the conversations over the radio are in Nepali. At one point Chongba tells me that as many as thirteen people are dead, all Sherpas. I can't believe what I am witnessing.

Towards the end of it all, Edita returns from the Icefall in a sombre mood. She disappears into the equipment tent without saying much to anyone. I think little of it, but when she doesn't emerge after a few minutes, I look in there to see how she is. I find her slumped on top of a kit bag, totally distraught.

Her friend Margaret is standing outside, so I grab hold of her and bundle her into the tent. I go to the kitchen tent and fetch tea for both of them as Margaret listens to Edita's story.

One of the fallen is Dorje Khatri – not our sirdar Dorje, but the sirdar of another team, Madison Mountaineering. He was a close relation of Ang Gelu from our own team, but Edita also knew him well. When I return with the tea she relates the story to both of us.

'I reached the summit of Cho Oyu with Dorje as my Sherpa,' Edita says. 'It was my first high-altitude climbing experience, and Dorje was my teacher and mentor. He gave me lots of confidence and even called me Sherpa, as he thought I was a strong climber.'

She explains that yesterday she went to say hello to him at the Madison Mountaineering camp. He was busy when she arrived, but he made time for her, sat her down, and offered her tea and coffee with a big smile.

'He said to me: "Edita, I was given a second life." Last summer he survived an avalanche on Himlung. Four of his friends were killed. I said to him, "Dorje, you've got a new life and you have to make the best out of it. Please, look after yourself." I don't know why I said this to him yesterday. He laughed, gave me a smile and a big hug. We chatted a bit more, but I knew he had work to do, so we said goodbye.'

She pauses, fighting back tears. Margaret gives her a hug, and I leave the tent to give them some privacy.

Later Edita tells us that, on the way down from the summit of Cho Oyu, she asked Dorje if she could help carry empty oxygen bottles. He laughed, but gave her a bottle anyway. After Cho Oyu he became her friend, and she felt like a sister to him. Last year, when she climbed Everest from the north side, Dorje was there with another team. When she was descending from Camp 3 after the summit, she was tired and got lost in the sprawl of Camp 2 on the North Ridge. Dorje spotted her and took her to his tent. He gave her tea and adjusted her oxygen bottle. She left with renewed energy and descended another 1,400m to the safety of Advanced Base Camp.

Shortly before lunch, Phil returns from the Icefall with our six brave Sherpas. By now most of the work has been done. Phil says Dorje and Ang Gelu supervised the work at the avalanche site, while Pasang Ongchu, Kami, Kusang and Samden helped to dig out many of the bodies. The avalanche swept several Sherpas down a crevasse beneath a ladder section, piling snow on top of them. The injuries were severe. The ladder was close to the serac that fell off the West Shoulder, and many of the dead were encased in ice. It must have been grim work, traumatic, and hard to comprehend.

Meanwhile Ricardo also made himself useful. He wandered over to the Himalayan Rescue Association tent to see if they needed help. David Hamilton of Jagged Globe put him to work treating injuries. Two were critical, some had broken limbs, and there were many lacerations from shards of ice.

For most of lunch we sit shell-shocked in total silence. Phil tells us thirteen Sherpas are confirmed dead, but as many as seven are still missing. It's an unprecedented tragedy, one of the most horrendous days in Everest's history.

There have been similar tragedies on the mountains of

Asia over the years, but not many. Sixteen members of a German team were buried in their sleep in an avalanche on 8,125m Nanga Parbat in 1937. An avalanche on Kang Guru, a 6,981m peak in the Annapurna region of Nepal, killed eighteen people in 2005. By far the worst, in terms of numbers, occurred on 7,134m Peak Lenin in Kyrgyzstan in 1990. Forty-five climbers were camped on the mountain when a vast serac wiped out their camp. Only two survived.

As for accidents on Everest, eight westerners died in a storm in 1996, and in both 2006 and 2012 there were around a dozen deaths in separate incidents across the season. In 1922 seven Sherpas died in an avalanche below the North Col. George Mallory and Howard Somervell both survived that avalanche. In his diary Somervell lamented the fact that no 'sahibs' died, which would have enabled them to share the loss in the same way they shared the risk.

I realise that today has been Everest's worst accident by some margin. It takes me some time to absorb this thought. When I woke up this morning I was anticipating my first climb into the fabled Khumbu Icefall. What I ended up doing was witnessing Everest's worst ever tragedy. I can't quite believe it.

We retire to our tents to contemplate the unimaginable. I assume Phil will cancel happy hour, but at four o'clock he is keen to round us up. We sit in solidarity for what we now call 'cocktail hour'. There is nothing to be happy about today.

Still, we are subdued. We speak little and sit in sombre silence for much of the time. There is no talk of leaving the mountain from a single one of us. We all want to stay, but some who have phoned home say their families are pressuring them to leave.

The gulf in perspective between climbers here on the

mountain and those left at home is like an ocean. For non-climbers, it is inconceivable that we should stay. We have seen many people die. Surely we understand that it's no longer safe, and we must end our expeditions out of respect for the dead?

They don't understand that we think about safety all the time, and we have other ways of showing our respect. How can we *not* think about these things, after seeing what we have today?

I can only give the climber's perspective. We accept the risk of death, though none of us wishes it, and we do all we can to avoid it. But accidents are frequent on dangerous Himalayan peaks. There are fatalities on Everest every year. They sometimes cause people to think again, but most of us have thought about those things already. We wouldn't be here if we hadn't weighed the risk and accepted it.

As for respect for the dead, why do people assume that the dead would want us to stop climbing? No climber I know would wish for companions to give up after they are gone. Every Sherpa knows that it's important to continue, because they all have families to feed. While many climbers abandon their expeditions after a fatality, this is a personal decision, and everyone is free to make up their own mind. This unwritten rule of climbing is sometimes difficult for those who are not climbers to understand.

Even so, we have all seen what the Icefall can do. Is it more dangerous now than it was before? This is my first time here. I don't know the answer to that, but many here have more experience. The decision about what happens next is in the hands of the Sherpas. None of us will force them to climb if they don't want to.

This question hangs in the air, but our team has a past history to draw on. Two years ago, on Manaslu, many of our team survived an avalanche that killed ten westerners and one Sherpa. They were in Camp 2 when a blast of air from the tumbling snow uprooted their tents and threw them several metres. They were boiling water for breakfast when they felt themselves catapulted down the slope, still inside their tents. By a miracle they all survived with only a few bruises. Kevin and Mel chose to go home for different reasons, Kevin because he had lost a boot.

Phil and Edita were there too. Both stayed, and Edita summited a couple of weeks later. More importantly there were the Sherpas; Dorje was also at Camp 2 when it happened, but most were down at Base Camp. Many of the senior Sherpas, including Dorje, Pasang Ongchu, Tarke, Chongba and Kami, decided to stay. There was no talk of leaving the mountain – they all wanted to reach the summit.

We have faith in our guys. But at six o'clock, shortly before dinner, an incident makes us realise that darker things are afoot.

We are sitting in the dining tent when we hear chanting outside. Phil and Robert are sitting near the door and go out to investigate. They see what Robert later describes as a mob of angry Sherpas from other teams passing by our camp.

'What's going on?' he says to Phil.

'It's nothing.'

'Don't bullshit me.'

They both come inside and sit down, but a moment later Dorje arrives and takes Phil outside again.

When Phil returns he explains what they've witnessed. He says a group of younger Sherpas from the IMG team, including a young ringleader employed by Jagged Globe, have just been through camp. They were agitating for Sherpas from all teams to go on strike.

We have a few older heads among our Sherpa team, chief among them Dorje. Dorje, Tarke and Chongba are all in their forties and hard as nails. They have many Everest and other 8,000m summits between them. There is no chance they would be influenced by young bucks in other teams. But to avoid an awkward situation, Dorje suggests to Phil that two of our Sherpas join the mob to provide an appearance of solidarity. He sends our young climbing sirdar Pasang Ongchu. Pasang is one of only about twenty Sherpas in Nepal with UIAGM certification, the top international qualification for mountain guides. Only a handful of these Sherpas are working on Everest this year, and this gives Pasang a high status. He is cheerful and helpful, and no militant. It's a good decision by Dorje.

I worry about Edita. I sit next to her at dinner, and she is taking her friend Dorje Khatri's death hard. They stood on the summit of Cho Oyu together. Dorje took her under his wing when other members of the team were flagging. He recognised that she was strong enough to reach the top, despite her inexperience. He was one of the older Sherpas, like our Dorje, and commanded respect from the younger crowd.

She keeps a blog of her own and I suggest that she posts a tribute to him. Although it's not much, it's something, and more than many of those who died today will receive. Memories are one of the best ways of helping a family through difficult times.

I am one of the last to leave the dining tent after dinner to head for my sleeping bag. As I'm passing the Sherpa dining tent – the place that has been declared out of bounds to inji (foreigners) for the duration of the expedition – Phil and Dorje emerge from inside.

'Hey, Mark, come in,' Phil says. 'The Sherpas would like us to join them tonight. Who else has gone back to their tents? Ask them to come and join us.'

I walk down the stone stairs built out of moraine blocks, linking the dining and storage tents with our sleeping tents, which are lower down in a slight trough. I shout to two figures I see wandering around in the darkness, and tell them that the Sherpas have invited us into their sanctum.

I return to the Sherpa dining tent and find that most of my teammates are already there. The room is more Spartan than ours, as you would expect. Benches line the perimeter and there are five or six tables to eat at. This is the place where twenty-three climbing Sherpas and seven kitchen staff come to relax and eat.

I'm embarrassed when half a dozen of them stand up as soon as I enter, offering me their seats.

'No, no, no,' I say, gesturing for them to sit down.

I squeeze in beside my old friend Chongba. I am given a shot of rum, and somebody arrives with tins of Tuborg beer. Many of our companions have lost friends and family today, but the evening is good-spirited, and they could not be more welcoming to us. I feel like there is no 'us and them'. Tonight we are united as a team, and share in the sense of loss.

'Do you still want to climb Lhotse?' I ask Chongba.

He will be my climbing Sherpa for the third time on summit day, should we be granted an opportunity. I know this could be a difficult question. When he replies, I study him carefully to see if there is any awkwardness.

He speaks only a few words of English, but it's enough.

'No problem,' he says, raising his glass with a big grin. His answer is immediate and as genuine as could be.

One of the highlights of the evening is when Ian launches into some impromptu theatre. He is describing the behaviour of a guide from another commercial operator. He decides the best way is by stagecraft. The guide had wandered officiously through the place where we stood at the end of the glacier as events were unfolding. None of our team had seen him before, or knew who he was.

'OK, we have a rescue to carry out here. Who has water?' Ian says, looking at Jay.

Jay takes the cue, and passes over a one-litre Nalgene bottle. Ian takes a sip, then strikes the bottle against the table.

'You better not drink that, I have a bug,' he says, passing the bottle back to Jay.

Acting is not Ian's forte, and nor is this behaviour in his character. This makes it all the more entertaining and everyone laughs. The performance makes no sense whatsoever, but several members of the team confirm the incident took place exactly as Ian described. They tell us that a cameraman from the Discovery Channel was following him, and the guide must have been suffering from an unusual case of stage fright as he played to the camera.

Later on, Phil introduces the four new members of the 'Junkies Family'. These are Peter, Jay, Caroline and Ricardo, the only members of the team who have not been on an Altitude Junkies expedition before. When he gets to Ricardo he introduces him as a 'guide'. He pronounces the word like it's some grand title used as a substitute for something more mundane. He gestures inverted commas in the air with his fingers.

Phil is quite adamant that his expeditions are unguided. He makes frequent references to mountain guides with expansive egos whose abilities fall short of the Sherpas. Everyone roars with laughter, but Ricardo takes it in good heart.

Ang Gelu is perhaps the most boisterous. He sits next to Edita. They share in the loss of Dorje Khatri – Edita as friend and Ang Gelu as family – and there is a natural bond between them.

He is talking about me to the others, and he keeps

calling me Mark Dickson, the name of our friend he helped to the summit of Everest two years ago.

'I'm not Mark Dickson,' I repeat every time he says it.

The other Sherpas find this funny, but Ang Gelu ignores me and keeps going. After a while, they all catch on, and join in.

'He's not Mark Dickson!' they cry in unison.

I tell them that I don't mind, because Ang Gelu helped me up the Second Step two years ago by offering me his hand.

'But he still doesn't remember my name!' I say, in mock hurt.

They find this Sherpa-Inji role reversal entertaining. I think back to the discussions we had a few days ago, about whether Ang Gelu should carry loads, and I wonder about his relationship with the rest of them.

Several drinks later it feels like well past midnight and I should be dragging myself off to bed. When I look at my watch I see that it's only 9.30.

It's been a strange day, a sad day, but it has ended in good spirit.

But the horrors of the last hours hit me again as I'm walking back to my tent. I wonder whether we should be drowning our sorrows like we did, when so many have lost so much. Maybe we should have paid our respects in silence. We were all affected by what we saw today; it will remain with us for a long time. For those who have lost family or friends it may never go away.

Then I think of the smiling faces in the tent tonight. Some of those smiles hid a greater loss. But life and loss go hand in hand, and tonight we shared it as a group in a spirit of friendship and solidarity.

We know that any one of us could have been up in the Icefall when the avalanche fell. We are all grateful that we are still here, and able to continue with our lives.

DAY 17
A STORM BREWING

Saturday 19ᵗʰ of April, 2014 – Everest Base Camp, Nepal

Life at 5,270m has many disadvantages, but hangovers aren't among them. I don't know how many Sherpa rums they gave me yesterday, but after more than a week at high altitude we have many more red blood cells than when we arrived. Physically, this morning feels like any other.

Emotionally, things feel very different. There is a sombre mood in camp this morning. The Sherpas need a period of time to pay their respects to those who have died, and so do we. No one is in any hurry to make the next move, and this is likely to remain the case for a day or two.

I spend the first two hours of this morning writing a blog post on my iPhone. I describe the sad events we witnessed, paying my respects to those who died and Sherpas in general. Without them none of this would be possible, and they spend much more time exposed to the dangers of the Icefall than we do.

At eleven o'clock I leave camp and head in the direction of Gorak Shep. I hope to find 3G connectivity somewhere along the route so that I can send my post. The trail is full of trekkers moving like caterpillars. Many are too exhausted to notice someone coming the other way, and I have to divert across boulders to get around them. Every few hundred metres I check my phone, but at no point is there even a sniff of 3G.

As I approach Gorak Shep I meet many of my teammates coming the other way and heading back to Base Camp for lunch. First I see Ian and Kevin, then Jay and Caroline, then finally Robert.

I reach the small community of teahouses shortly after midday. I stand in the courtyard of each one in turn searching for connectivity, but there is nothing.

I get increasingly frustrated. I've come all this way just to press the send button, and soon I'm going to have to go all the way back again, all for no purpose. Can you imagine walking for an hour just to buy a pint of milk, but the store is closed, so you have to walk all the way back again? You've wasted two hours, and now you have nothing to pour on your breakfast cereal.

It's hard to feel any sympathy. These are what they call first-world problems. I queue at the salad bar for ten minutes, only to find they have no kumquat slices. I have a splinter on my thumb, and it's painful to tweet from my phone. My wallet is too small. I can't believe how hard it is to buy 100% organic wild boar sausage.

Yesterday sixteen people died in an avalanche. I watched their bodies being carried down to Base Camp. Sixteen families in the Khumbu will be poorer this year. Their children may have to quit school to find work. All of them will be overwhelmed with grief this morning, and here I am worrying about 3G connectivity. Two hours of my time, in this easy-paced expedition life, is nothing at all. I should be happy for the trouble.

Lots of other trekkers are hanging around fiddling with their phones. Most of them only arrived this morning, and they didn't see what I saw yesterday. I'm ashamed of myself.

I'm running out of time if I want to get back to Base Camp in time for a one o'clock lunch. I bomb it back at a pace I would never have believed possible a week ago – a speed otherwise known as 'Kevin's Pace'.

The first part of the trail back to Base Camp weaves up and down on stony ground. Scores of trekkers bar my way. I have no choice but to race past them, boulder-hopping on rocks beside the trail. Often they are so unaware of my presence that their trekking poles flip out in front of me, tripping me up. I sidestep them and skip past, and still they don't notice me.

These overtaking manoeuvres are exhausting on the uphill sections. I keep reaching the brow of a rise gasping for breath, but I soldier on at the same pace – a pace that would have been dangerous when we first came to Base Camp. Overexertion like this would have brought on altitude sickness for sure. But now I'm so well acclimatised that I feel like I'm just having a good workout.

The ridge of moraine approaching Base Camp is easier going. I catch up with Robert just beyond the end of it, and we complete the walk together, arriving for dinner with five minutes to spare.

The things I do for my dinner. I'm tired and dripping with sweat. They all laugh at my ragged appearance when I enter the dining tent, but I'm pleased I made it.

I'm frustrated I haven't been able to send my blog post. I know the media will be having a field day about the avalanche. They will be printing lies and half-truths without trying to understand the many nuances. I wanted to put forward a true picture of what happened before too many inaccuracies get propagated as fact. Once these myths circulate in one publication, they get picked up by another, and before long everyone takes the myths as truth. Once that happens it's difficult to reel the falsehoods back in again.

Our lack of internet access means that, happily, we are protected from the media storm that I'm sure has accompanied this tragedy. I've seen enough in the past to be able to predict the headlines, though. Rich western tourists send Sherpas to their deaths to satisfy their egos and tick off their bucket list by climbing Everest.

While there is an element of truth in this it's only a tiny fraction of the full story. Journalists who write these headlines have not been here and looked up into the Icefall with their boots on, ready to go up. They don't understand the motivations of mountaineers (both Sherpa and westerner) and the calculated risks we all take to do what we enjoy.

Nor do they have an appreciation of the historical background that has led to Sherpas becoming the tigers of Himalayan mountaineering. Many Sherpas moved to Darjeeling in the early 20th century to gain work with mountaineering expeditions. They quickly became indispensable, and there have been few Himalayan expeditions since in which they haven't played an integral part. On Everest a team of Sherpas known as the Icefall Doctors fixes the route through the Khumbu Icefall every year. Sherpas take great pride in fixing the route up the Lhotse Face. Far from being forced to do it by westerners, they will not allow others to trespass on what they see as their territory.

After this tragedy some teams will remain on the mountain and others will pack up and leave. These decisions will be based on the wishes of the Sherpas, as we all know we cannot climb the mountain without them. Chomolungma belongs to the Sherpas – it's only right they have an increasing say in what happens here. But the history of Everest has involved Sherpas and westerners working hand in hand, and the future of Everest will be better if this remains the case. This is the way Friday's sad events should be treated: not by apportioning blame, but by trying our best to share the loss some of us feel more keenly than others.

It's atrocious weather in the afternoon, snowing and cold, and all we can do is huddle in our tents. At happy hour I'm quiet for a different reason. Robert plays music on his iPod of an era and style that only Kevin and Louis are familiar with – but boy are they familiar with it. The rest of us listen in silence.

There are rumours that some of the teams who lost Sherpas will be giving up their expeditions and leaving the mountain. Alpine Ascents, Adventure Consultants and Jagged Globe all lost team members, but nothing is confirmed yet. We learn that the ringleader of the Sherpa protesters is a guide called Pasang Tenzing, Jagged Globe's sirdar. Some of our Sherpas tell us that IMG's Sherpas were prominent in the protest yesterday. But with a mob like that, it's difficult to know who is a troublemaker, and who is just being carried along in the flow.

Phil looks stressed and downcast, but Dorje is being very supportive. Our own Sherpas are not getting involved, as far as I can tell. Those I spoke to today are all prepared to continue once the trouble has passed. Ian is upbeat at dinner tonight and being his usual positive self, helping to lighten the mood. He is confident that everything will be OK.

DAY 18
THE SHERPA SUMMONS

Sunday 20ᵗʰ of April , 2014 – Everest Base Camp, Nepal

We have another discussion about the Sherpa situation at breakfast. We know we can't climb the mountain without them, and rumours of a possible strike are growing stronger. Many Sherpas have gone home to be with their families, including those from Russell Brice's Himex team, who are camping just a short distance away. Although these particular Sherpas intend to return after a few days, there are others who may not.

Under the circumstances no reputable western operator will force their Sherpas to climb if they don't want to. But we need enough of them to stay for rope fixing to the summit to be practical. We also need the Icefall Doctors to keep the ever-changing route through the Khumbu Icefall open, a job that now looks more dangerous.

Ricardo's enthusiasm is extraordinary, but there are times when it's a little unrealistic. I took my hat off to him on Friday for volunteering at the medical tent and doing some useful work there. It's something I would never have thought of doing myself.

'What can we do to help the Sherpas?' he says at breakfast. 'I'm happy to do some extra load carrying, or if anything needs to be done on the Lhotse Face I can help fix rope.'

I tell him what happened last year when western climbers interfered with rope fixing on the Lhotse Face. After Ueli Steck and Simone Moro had their little disagreement with Sherpas high on the mountain, the latter downed tools and returned to Camp 2. Thinking that he was being helpful, Ueli Steck picked up the rope and fixed the next hundred metres of line. This did not go down well. The two Europeans were confronted by an angry Sherpa mob, and they fled down to Base Camp in fear of their lives.

'I don't think it's a good idea to help the Sherpas fix the ropes, Ricardo,' I say. 'Or help with carrying loads. It's best to wait and see what happens.'

But I have cause to thank Ricardo. He seems to be the member of the team most adept at seeking out 3G and Wi-Fi (although Edita challenges him in this regard). After breakfast he and I head out to Gorak Shep to have another go at sending my blog post.

We amble along the moraine, arriving in just over an hour. Expeditions are a chance to escape the stresses and absurdities of modern life, but with the Sherpa politics developing at Base Camp it doesn't seem that way at the moment. Ricardo doesn't help by spending much of the walk talking about politics and religion.

We reach Gorak Shep at 10.30. Ricardo heads straight to a smaller teahouse called the Yeti. It is tucked away behind the others, and I would never have found it on my own. The place is quieter than the more visible teahouses, and the Wi-Fi is pretty quick. We pay 800 rupees for an hour (about $8 US). I send my post, then check messages on various channels, including Hotmail, Gmail, Twitter, Facebook and my WordPress blog. I was expecting to be bombarded with messages of concern, but only four people made any reference to the avalanche. This goes to show that most of my friends have no idea where I am. I expect most of those who do know I'm climbing a mountain called Lhotse don't know how close to Everest it is. Or they know where I am, but they don't give a toss. Yes, that's probably it.

After an hour of surfing I leave Ricardo where he is and head back to camp. Although I give myself plenty of time to amble back, the trail is clogged up with snail-paced trekkers. I have no option but to race past them at Kevin's pace again.

All appears peaceful at Base Camp, but beneath the surface things are stirring

Back at camp the plot thickens. Our Sherpas have been summoned to an emergency meeting with all the other Sherpas at Base Camp. They are going to discuss what to do next in the wake of the avalanche. Expedition leaders and operators are not invited, but his business depends on the outcome, so Phil goes to the meeting and lurks at a discreet distance with his friend Russell Brice.

When he returns he describes the atmosphere as intimidating. One Indian climber tried to argue with them and was nearly lynched. Westerners who tried to take photographs were singled out for abuse. Phil says the ringleaders were Pasang Tenzing of Jagged Globe, and another Sherpa he didn't recognise who was wearing a purple beanie.

Dorje later confirms that the Sherpa leaders produced a list of demands for the government, including a petition which all Sherpas were asked to sign.

The demands were:

1. More compensation for the families of the victims;[2]
2. Improved insurance for Sherpas working on Everest;
3. Helicopter evacuation for insured Sherpas;
4. To cancel this year's Everest season and go home.

The first three demands are reasonable. Phil tells me the second two had already been met before the expedition, though the Sherpa leaders appeared to be unaware of it.

It's the fourth demand that is controversial, and could have strong repercussions. Operators would face big losses, and the sacrifices the rest of us have made to be here – in time, energy, work and family commitments, not to mention huge amounts of money – would all be for very little. It will have an impact on the Sherpa and tourist economy in future years. There were many bad headlines about Sherpa mob rule after last year's fight at Camp 2. If they go on strike then this reputation will become firmer.

Our own Sherpas were present at the meeting but did not sign the petition. Even so, Phil is downcast when we meet for happy hour.

'That guy Pasang Tenzing is up to his old tricks again. He's trying to get all the Sherpas from other teams to go home, just like he did on Manaslu.'

It's news to me that Sherpas threatened to strike after the avalanche on Manaslu in 2012. On that occasion eleven people died. Phil says there were protests, and a few teams had to end their expeditions because of it, but there was no blanket strike.

Kevin, Mel and Edita were all on Manaslu two years ago. Mel even witnessed Pasang Tenzing agitating for Sherpas to leave.

'You remember him, Mel?' Phil says.

Mel laughs. He puts his palms together, mimicking Pasang's style.

This year the loss of life has been borne by the Sherpa community. But Edita points out that on Manaslu the fatalities were mainly westerners. Only one Sherpa was among the dead, yet still there was a small core of Sherpas agitating for everybody to go home.

The mood around the table is subdued. Then Jay, who has been silent for most of the session, suddenly pipes up.

'Heck, even if the Sherpas do go home, we'll be all right. We got Ricardo. He said this morning he was going to fix ropes on the Lhotse Face.'

We roar with laughter.

Unwittingly, Ian also helps to lighten the mood this happy hour. He is our industrial-quantity drinker, but he is now on antibiotics for a cough. This means he is unable to drink for a few days. Most evenings he is the person who finishes his red wine first. He takes our order and goes to the kitchen tent to ask Da Pasang for the next round, but not tonight. When Da Pasang brings in a tray with the second batch of drinks, he refuses to believe that no glass is for Ian. He keeps putting a glass in front of him, and Ian keeps waving him away. If I didn't know Da

Pasang better, I would suspect he was making fun of him.

'No, Da Pasang, thank you. It's OK,' Ian says with his usual politeness. 'I don't want one today.'

He does want one, but he can't, and it's killing him. Meanwhile I am crying with laughter.

'Ian, I promise I didn't ask Da Pasang to do that,' I say.

But I might have done if I'd thought of it.

DAY 19
RUMOURS

Monday 21ˢᵗ of April, 2014 – Everest Base Camp, Nepal

At one point last night I heard angry Sherpa voices debating a few metres away from my tent. Jay heard it too, and this morning we discuss what it means.

'Hopefully it was one of the Sherpa agitators arguing with our guys, rather than our guys arguing among themselves,' Jay says.

But Phil is more downcast than ever at breakfast. The stresses of the last few days have taken their toll on him.

'Pasang Tenzing has done what he wanted. IMG's Sherpas are leaving, and Dorje says some of our Sherpas want to leave now too.'

Our Sherpas have always greeted me warmly as I've walked around camp over the last couple of days. On the surface our relationship has remained the same, and nothing much has changed, but this may be because the Sherpas I know well are the older ones. They have been working for Phil for longer, and are the most loyal. Phil believes most of them still want to stay, but if a critical mass of Sherpas from other teams ends up leaving then things could fall apart quickly. Every departure from another team tests the loyalty of our guys, making Dorje's job harder.

Our Sherpas are great; I've seen them in action on many previous expeditions. But they can't fix the Khumbu Icefall, Lhotse Face and summit ridge on their own. It requires 10,000m of rope for a start. We need a few teams to stick around, or it's going to be impossible to continue.

'This thing's becoming a shit show,' Phil says. 'The dominoes are falling over, and our boys can't stay if the rest of the Sherpa community leaves. I've told Dorje if we quit now that's the end of Manaslu and Cholatse in the fall, maybe even Everest next year. I've got 1,000 kilograms of equipment in the Western Cwm. If we end up having to leave it there then Trish and I may have to file for bankruptcy.'

It's been a stressful time for Phil and I'm sure he is under a lot of financial pressure to keep going, but I don't believe things are quite as bad as he imagines. Sometimes expeditions don't go to plan. Usually we climb higher than we have here, for sure, and on most mountains it's the weather that stops us, rather than human frailty. But in both cases the expedition fails because of things outside our control. That's part and parcel of mountaineering.

Emotions are running high at the moment. The Sherpa agitators don't seem to be aware that they are shooting themselves in the foot. Whether this year's Everest season can still be salvaged we don't know. But it's just one season, and common sense and the natural order have to prevail in the end.

We have a pessimistic discussion over breakfast. The situation, as described by Phil, suggests there is little chance of the season continuing. Too many Sherpas will be leaving to make a route up both Everest and Lhotse practical.

The bigger picture is that there are already a smaller number of tourists in the Khumbu this year. If this season gets cancelled because of a fatal avalanche and a Sherpa strike, then the outlook for next year looks gloomy too. Some of the team members are talking as if it's the end of mountaineering in Nepal. Things aren't quite as bleak as that, but it's possible some operators will pull out for a few years.

We can foresee this, and so can the older, wiser Sherpas like Dorje, but the youngsters don't understand. More cynical members of our team say that they are just looking for an excuse to quit work and get paid for it. We are unanimous that our own Sherpas should receive full pay whatever happens. We know that none of this is their fault, and there is no reason they should suffer for it.

My feeling is that, if the season gets cancelled, then sixteen people will have died in vain. It's the Sherpa mountaineers who have raised the Sherpa people above the norm and made them great. Since they moved to Darjeeling to work with expeditions, they have worked hand in hand with western mountaineers over the years, sharing the losses and risks to varying degrees. This year the loss was theirs; on Manaslu westerners bore the brunt of the tragedy. We shouldn't let these changing fortunes drive a wedge between the two communities.

It's Sherpa mountaineers who have made the Khumbu region prosperous in comparison to the rest of Nepal. Many Sherpas own teahouses and trekking agencies now, and they can afford to send their children to good schools. They gain qualifications. Some become teachers, and there are even some doctors. This trajectory is continuing, and those who died in the Icefall on Friday are part of that tradition. That's not to say we shouldn't do more to prevent these disasters – they have also become a part of Sherpa history. But we need to draw positives from tragedy, for each one can be a lesson too, and have a silver lining. It would be sad if the great tradition of Sherpa mountaineers takes a setback because of the actions of a few. It would compound the tragedy if the Sherpa community loses much of the goodwill that has built up over the years.

We are gloomy over breakfast, but better news emerges as the morning goes on. Before breakfast IMG's climbing sirdar told Phil that their Sherpas wanted to leave. Later in the morning Robert goes over to speak to IMG's expedition leader Greg Vernovage. There he meets Ang Jangbu Sherpa, a wealthy Nepali who owns a company called Beyul Adventure. They are the local agency that IMG subcontract their expeditions to.

'Your sirdar told our leader your Sherpas are leaving,' Robert tells him.

Ang Jangbu turns and pats his chest.

'I'm the sirdar!' he says.

IMG are key to whether the season continues. They are a huge team, with around fifty Sherpas. If they stay, then the rope fixing will happen, and everybody's expedition can continue.

Expedition base camps are hives of rumour and gossip. Very little information can be relied upon. Another rumour reaches us that Alpine Ascents have 'definitely' confirmed they are leaving. They lost seven Sherpas in the avalanche, so it would be no surprise if it were true, and no one would begrudge them this decision. It would be difficult to continue after such a loss of personnel. More importantly, in these circumstances it would be the right thing to do.

We believe this news is more reliable, because we receive it directly from its source. Two Alpine Ascents clients come over to ask if they can join our team. None of us knows who they are, and Phil is sympathetic, but he feels duty bound to turn down their request. He has hired resources for seven Everest climbers and five Lhotse climbers. With two more members these resources would be stretched.

Other good news arrives with a message from Phil's wife Trish. She tells him that Nepal's Ministry of Tourism has said it will accept most of the demands in the petition. The only item likely to be rejected is the one calling for expeditions to be cancelled – of course this would be unacceptable to them. If they cancel the season before anyone has climbed out of Base Camp, the local climbing agencies might sue them, demanding the return of permit fees, Icefall Doctor fees, and liaison officer salaries. Expeditions must pay the government these expenses. Permit fees alone earn the government over $2 million a year. Very little of this windfall filters down the chain, and this is one of the things fuelling discontent. The Ministry of Tourism has a reputation for incompetence, but even they must realise such a thing would be harmful for tourism.

Our evening ends on a bizarre, worrying note that might have put Sherpa politics into perspective.

Mel doesn't arrive for dinner, and nobody knows where he is. At first no one is concerned. We know he has Chinese friends in other teams. As an artist and photographer, he has often stayed out after dark to film the lights of Base Camp penetrating through tent fabric. But by the time we finish dinner and head off to bed, he still hasn't returned. Some of the team become a little worried about him, and this worries the rest of us too.

Robert and Peter say they saw him leave camp with his pack at two o'clock. A couple of our Sherpas then say they spotted a lone figure above the second ladder of the Icefall at 2.30.

'No, he wouldn't go into the Icefall alone!' Edita says. 'When we started walking through the Icefall after the avalanche, Mel wouldn't cross the first ladder. He is too cautious.'

Besides, he would need to be a superman to reach the

second ladder of the Icefall from camp in only half an hour.

'If he's gone into the Icefall on his own then he's clearly deranged. In which case we've got sod all chance of finding him,' I say, making my own diplomatic contribution.

It didn't come out quite the way I'd intended. I meant to suggest that I was quite sure Mel wouldn't be stupid enough to go there on his own. The figure must have been someone else. The darkness of evening in Everest Base Camp isn't the time for sarcasm, though, and other team members are still imagining the worst.

But Robert and a handful of Sherpas bring the evening to a happy conclusion when they walk out of camp in the direction of Gorak Shep. They've not gone far when they notice someone a few metres off the trail making signals with the light of their mobile phone. It's Mel. He had underestimated the amount of time it would take to get to Kala Pattar and back, and lost his way navigating the trail in the dark without a head torch.

With our mini drama over, we go to sleep and prepare ourselves for a fresh batch of Sherpa politics tomorrow.

DAY 20
RALLY

Tuesday 22nd of April, 2014 – Everest Base Camp, Nepal

There is no fresh news to report over breakfast for a change, but a puja will take place at ten o'clock this morning. The mountain gods are angry, and we need to appease them again. It's also an opportunity to remember those who died in the avalanche on Friday.

Phil keeps encouraging me to wander across camp and talk to our friends at Jagged Globe. I've climbed with both of their leaders, and as we left Lobuche I chatted to some of their clients. There are plenty of rumours flying around camp, many concerning their sirdar, Pasang Tenzing. Phil is interested in news from their side and hopes it will clarify matters. I'm not so sure.

He is a bit more upbeat this morning about the season continuing as planned. He believes if Sherpa agitators like Pasang Tenzing are removed from camp then the atmosphere will be different. Perhaps so, but if he's harbouring any ideas that I might wander over there and talk them into sending him home then he's being a little far-fetched. He might as well ask me to fix the rest of the route through the Icefall while I'm up there.

The puja takes place outside the tent of the Sagarmatha Pollution Control Committee (SPCC). This is the organisation that employs the Icefall Doctors to maintain the route up to the Western Cwm. As their name implies, the SPCC's main priority is to look after the environment in the Khumbu region, but a few years ago they were looking for a way to get more funding. The Everest season brings millions of dollars into the Khumbu region every year. For two months hundreds of cooks, porters, climbing Sherpas and teahouse owners earn a good seasonal income. The SPCC wanted a piece of the action, and they came up with the idea of employing a team of climbing Sherpas to maintain the route through the Icefall.

This role is now official. As part of the expedition paperwork, every team pays a fee for the Icefall Doctors, currently set at around $600 per climber. Four hundred climbing permits are issued in an average Everest season, which means the Icefall Doctor licence earns the SPCC a quarter of a million dollars every spring.

The environment in the Khumbu region is a worthy cause, but not everybody is happy with the arrangement. Many teams believe their own Sherpas would do a better job of fixing the route. And most of the $600 Icefall Doctor fee doesn't actually go towards maintaining the route through the Icefall. Instead the SPCC puts it into their pot for other projects.

We leave shortly after 9.30. The SPCC tent is just above the main trail through camp. When we get there we find that, for some unexplained reason, the puja is taking place indoors. A raised area of moraine just above the entrance to the tent provides a natural grandstand. Dozens of people crowd onto it, but most of those mingling around are unable to see anything.

One of the first people we bump into when we arrive is Chris, Jagged Globe's assistant leader. Ian attempted Manaslu with him in 2008. I met him back in 2005 when he was my leader on Aconcagua, the highest mountain in

South America.

One of Jagged Globe's Sherpas was killed in Friday's avalanche. Chris is honest about the difficulties they find themselves facing, perhaps more than he would be with his clients. I don't know whether this is because he trusts us to keep it to ourselves or because we have news we can give him in return. Not wishing to tiptoe around the issues, I ask him a direct question about Pasang Tenzing. He is of course aware of Pasang's role as one of the ringleaders. He believes other members of their Sherpa team may be involved as well. It's difficult for him, because he wants to continue with their expedition too; and Jagged Globe are as reliant on their Sherpas as we are, so they can't just get rid of their sirdar. It would almost certainly cause a mutiny, and that would mean the end for them.

I've travelled with Jagged Globe on many occasions, and I'm sorry to see the support of their local Nepali agency unravelling in this way. They don't deserve this. I wonder how much they knew of Pasang Tenzing's past history as a troublemaker. When you're taking $50,000 or more from each of your clients, you don't want one of your staff sabotaging the expedition. If they knew about it, I would have expected them to act sooner. They have trusted and supported him over a number of years, and there was a time when he was a loyal member of their team.

I don't see much of the puja as I stand behind a crowd of people listening to the chanting. After about an hour I have a coughing fit and retreat down the hill to an area of rocks where there is fresher air. It's much more peaceful sitting there on my own. I'm in a better position to observe the proceedings and contemplate what all of it means.

As I'm staring into space I notice a Sherpa in a colourful buff making his way towards me. When he is still a few metres away I recognise him as Dawa, a qualified mountain guide I have travelled with on two previous expeditions.

When I climbed Mera and Island Peak with Dawa a few years ago he carried a copy of Nepal's draft constitution for bedtime reading. He is working for a Malaysian team this year. As a Sherpa with an interest in politics I wonder if he is involved in any of the intrigue this year, but as I talk to him it becomes clear that he is staying out of it. Like the vast majority of Sherpas, he just wants to get on with the climb.[3]

We move forward again for the final part of the ceremony. Once again I can't see much, and I listen to the chanting in silence. When it finishes a voice begins speaking in Nepali, then another in English. The names of a few western expedition leaders are mentioned but I can hear nothing else of what is being said.

I move downhill and stand on a large rock that gives me a better view, though I still can't hear clearly. I realise that a few Sherpas are making demands again. The main speaker is the man in the purple beanie whom Phil told us about a couple of days ago.[4]

The great and the good of western operators are invited to come forward and speak. Russell Brice, David Breashears and Dave Hahn all take their turn, but none of them are great orators – or at least not in this context. Most of them just mutter a few platitudes in English and pay their respects to those who have died. Under the circumstances it's the only thing they can do.

I feel sick. The puja is being used by a few militant Sherpas to stage another rally and make demands. This is not the forum to reach an agreement and resolve differences. A puja is supposed to be a religious ceremony to ask the mountain gods to grant safe passage. This one was also meant to be a memorial service for those who died, but now it's been hijacked.

At 12.15 I walk away and return to camp, totally downhearted.

With Pumori as a backdrop, a puja becomes a rally

Over lunch we discuss this reversal of fortunes. Most of us couldn't hear what was being said, but those who were a little closer confirmed my suspicions. The militant Sherpas, who want to cancel the season and go home, dominated the meeting. This created the misleading impression that the prevailing mood in camp is for giving up rather than fighting on. I wonder what has happened to the older, wiser heads like Dorje and Tarke – strong characters who command respect. There are plenty like them around camp, but they were taking a back seat at the ceremony. All the Sherpas involved in the action were young.

Meanwhile Phil has decided to take matters into his

own hands. With time running out, he and Russell Brice have arranged to take a helicopter to Kathmandu later today. Their aim is to meet with officials from the Ministry of Tourism. They hope to convince them to meet the Sherpas' more reasonable demands in return for persuading them to stay.

They also have a specific grievance to make against the ringleaders of the protests. They believe these people are bringing the industry, and Sherpas, into disrepute. This harms the livelihoods of western operators, and it also harms the hundreds of Nepali staff they employ.

The chopper will cost them $6,000. They hope to convince some of the owners of other mountaineering operators to join them and contribute to the cost. The owners of most of the big operators – IMG, Alpine Ascents, Adventure Consultants, Jagged Globe and RMI – are here in Nepal.

We're dispersing after lunch when Phil summons us back to the dining tent. He is very insistent, and we are sure it can only be bad news. What can he have heard so suddenly?

This impression is reinforced when he appears with Dorje. As he makes his announcement, our sirdar stands shoulder to shoulder in solidarity.

'Guys, while I'm away, please stay down at this end of camp and don't wander up to the other end. Russell Brice's clients have been physically threatened by Sherpas, and they've been given seven days to get out of Base Camp. It may be nothing, but we've requested the army to get up here and provide protection for ourselves, Himex and Asian Trekking. We're the three teams down here who want to stay, and the only ones whose Sherpas didn't sign the petition.'

This is becoming surreal. Have we stumbled into a war zone, or are we just climbing a mountain as we thought?

We gaze at each other across the table in numbed shock, unable to believe the direction this expedition is taking. What on earth did Russell Brice's clients say to provoke this? Or was it something Russell said during the meeting that caused the militant Sherpas to threaten his clients? Like the other western leaders, he expressed sympathy for the victims. But he was the only one to talk about the commercial implications of abandoning the mountain.

Russell had spoken the simple truth, but was it seen as a threat? If so, then threatening his clients is a cowardly reaction. What have they done to bring about this situation? Unlike us they don't have their own Sherpas to protect them. Russell allowed his Sherpas to return to Khumjung to see their families after the avalanche.

But before we've had time to absorb this bombshell, Phil drops another one. It's just as momentous, and could be more significant.

'It's not all bad news. Russell's liaison offer has told him that the government is going to announce that all the Sherpa demands will be met. But anyone who goes on strike will be banned from working on the top ten peaks in Nepal for life.'

Blimey. Two contrasting pieces of news if ever there were.

The first bit of news caught the government with their pants down. Earlier this year they announced they would be stationing police and army at Base Camp. It was a reaction to last year's Sherpa fight, and aimed at preventing precisely the sort of violent threats Phil just told us about. The announcement received a lot of coverage in the western media.

Unfortunately, like nearly everything the Ministry of Tourism announces, it didn't happen. There are no police or army stationed at Base Camp, and if they bring any up now they will not be acclimatised. They will only be coming up here to make themselves sick.

Phil's second bombshell needs to be taken with a few spoonfuls of salt. It could be true – perhaps Russell Brice's liaison officer did say all that, but that doesn't mean it will happen. Past history shows that Nepal's government is quite incapable of acting decisively.

Phil leaves on his chopper later in the afternoon, and before he goes he puts Robert in charge of happy hour. We hope this is because Robert is the best leader among us, rather than because he's a teetotaller.

Several of Phil's rules are immediately broken. Robert goes into the Sherpa dining tent to give them his iPad to watch a movie. This is definitely a good violation of the rules. Then Robert allows people to use their phones at the dinner table. This is a bad violation, and we have to tell Edita off for trying to watch a movie of her own during happy hour. Next, Ian is permitted by Robert to order a fifth glass of wine after dinner is over. This, of course, should never have counted as a violation in the first place.

But the strangest turn of events is when the meal transitions into Ricardo's karaoke night. Robert selects some retro tunes on his iPod and Ricardo sings along. It's novel enough to start with. Ricardo has an amazing voice. His performance is all the more commendable because we are at 5,270m and he's gasping for breath between lines.

But I start to lose interest some time after his rendition of The Beatles' *While My Guitar Gently Weeps*. He asks for requests, but my teammates seem to have decided it's only worth his while singing ballads. I disappear to my tent to fetch my water bottle. When I return to fill it from the flasks, he's singing Elton John's *Sorry Seems to Be the Hardest Word*.

It's been a sad day, and he has a great voice, but really – do we deserve this?

After the umpteenth minor chord I lose my mind and

burst into hysterical laughter.

'I can fetch a bucket if anyone wants to throw up?' I say in a loud voice.

There are some shocked faces around the table. But, true professional that he is, Ricardo keeps performing despite the heckling. I pat him on the shoulder and leave the tent, still laughing like a maniac.

DAY 21
ESCAPE TO THE HILLS

Wednesday 23rd of April, 2014 – Everest Base Camp, Nepal

There is nothing new to report this morning. For the first time in nearly a week we have an opportunity to escape the politics and enjoy the mountains. This is what we came for, after all.

After breakfast I set off for Pumori Camp 1 with Edita and Kevin. It's a little cloudy to begin with, and I don't know whether we will get the fantastic views of Everest and Lhotse that the viewpoint is known for. But we're keen to get out for some exercise, and we agree to climb as high as we can.

I lead the way, plodding like a tortoise, but we are all much better acclimatised now. We advance up the moraine ridge above Base Camp much more quickly than last time. It helps that we know the way, and can keep to the trail. The sun warms us through the clouds, and it's pleasant going.

As we approach Pumori Base Camp, where we turned around last time, I hear Edita speak behind me.

'I am so happy to be walking again.'

I know what she means. So many of the bad things in life have been disturbing our thoughts over the last week that we had almost forgotten where we are. As we trudge up the trail, among an amphitheatre of breathtaking peaks, all these things seem like they exist in another world. Life is nothing but simplicity again.

Mark during a happier moment on the walk up to Pumori Camp 1

We reach Pumori Camp 1 at 10.30, after an hour and a half of walking. An angry lenticular cloud hangs over the tops of Everest and Lhotse, but we can see enough of the Lhotse Face for me to trace our route until it disappears into grey.

There is a tall cairn here, and a ledge big enough for one or two tents. Someone has built a dry-stone wall to provide shelter from the wind. We are in the sun, and it's warm enough for us to remain here some time.

We can see right over the Lho La to the north side of Everest. Edita and I are able to point out Camp 3 on the North Face and two of the 'steps' to Kevin, though we're not sure which is which.

Edita discovers she can get 3G up here, and we take a selfie of the three of us with her phone. She posts it on Facebook there and then.

The clouds drift away to the north after we've been resting for half an hour. The full panorama is revealed, much to our delight, with the summits of both Everest and Lhotse visible at last. It's an unexpected gift, and by the time we have descended back to Base Camp we are feeling blessed to be here for the first time in nearly a week.

This feeling is reinforced over lunch when Robert receives a text message from Phil's wife Trish. She tells him to give her a call when he has a minute. He phones her immediately and puts her on speakerphone so that everyone around the dinner table can hear. Phil's voice comes on the line, and he describes the outcome of his meeting with the Ministry of Tourism.

He is upbeat, and tells us the Ministry have agreed to meet the majority of the Sherpa demands. They also reinforced the message that the season cannot be abandoned. They said that ringleaders like Jagged Globe's Pasang Tenzing would have their licences to work in tourism revoked.

'The Prime Minister wanted to talk to Russell and myself tomorrow,' he says casually, 'but we have to get back to Base Camp. A delegation from the Ministry is flying in to speak to the Sherpas.'

He sounds like a relieved man. It was an expensive trip for him, but we're pleased that it seems to have been worthwhile. He can't hear us, but we sit around the table applauding.

'Did I hear that right? Did he say he had to cancel a meeting with the Prime Minister?' Peter says after Robert has ended the call.

I have a hunch that part was bullshit, but the mood is good, so I don't say anything.

Call it a see-saw or a roller coaster, but the day isn't finished yet. There are a few more twists.

A New Zealand friend of Caroline's called Mark, who is climbing with IMG, comes over with another dispiriting piece of news. He tells her they have pulled the plug on their expedition. The reason given is that they can no longer guarantee the safety of their Sherpas.

'They think the Icefall is now too dangerous?'

'No,' he replies. 'They can't protect them from threats from other Sherpas.'

These threats are like a spider's web of intrigue. I'm yet to speak to anyone who has been threatened directly, but this doesn't make the threats themselves any less real. Is the mere existence of a few rumours enough to frighten people? So it seems, unless of course there is real substance behind them. It feels like I'm in some Monty Python sketch. Against these things the dangers of the Khumbu Icefall are starting to look like a more predictable risk.

Robert calls Phil immediately, and now Phil becomes utterly downcast.

'If IMG leave then we're all fucked.'

IMG have a huge complement of fifty or sixty experienced climbing Sherpas. If they leave then it's a major blow for all the teams who want to remain. We need Sherpa manpower to fix the route to the summit.

I get the impression that he feels let down by IMG after going to the trouble of pleading with the Ministry on behalf of all operators. He feels they could have waited twenty-four hours to hear the outcome of their visit to Base Camp, and its consequences, before quitting.

Later in the afternoon I see an angry Dorje stomping around camp with a furrowed frown.

'Are you OK, Dorje?' I ask.

'Tim Rippel come over to our camp, to Sherpa tent, and tell us "we are leaving". So I say to him "If you want to go, then go, but don't come over here and tell my Sherpa!"'

Tim Rippel is the owner of Peak Freaks, a small Canadian outfit. Their departure would hardly be significant to anyone else on the mountain, but every domino that falls runs the risk of toppling another one. Dorje has been working tirelessly to keep our team loyal, and he doesn't want any of those dominoes toppling near us. It's been easier for him here in the quiet end of camp. He's furious that Tim Rippel came all the way over here to announce his decision.

It's against Phil's rules to invite people from other teams into our dining tent. He believes that bugs get transmitted that way, and illnesses can be avoided if we keep ourselves in quarantine. He's not here, though, and we are all eager for news from the IMG camp. We agree to Caroline's suggestion to invite her friend Mark for a glass of wine.

He provides new information about the avalanche. I thought we were the only western witnesses to the tragedy, but this isn't true. Mark tells us that IMG's clients had also gone for a foray into the Icefall that morning. Unlike us, they left during darkness and were actually up there when it happened.

'We saw the avalanche come down, and it was total panic. Everybody started running down and coming down ladders. Then one of our guides, Austin, said it was OK and it was going to miss us. But still it was so big we were dusted by the snow. We were at the Football Field at the time and came down straight away. Austin went on up and said it was about another fifteen minutes before he reached the debris.'

'Only fifteen minutes?' I say in disbelief. 'That means you were fifteen minutes away from death!'

He gives a wry smile. 'Yeah, I guess so.'

This is significant. It means westerners shared the risk

with Sherpas that day. There could so easily have been western casualties as well. Would this have made any difference to the politics which has seeped through camp like a disease? Perhaps, but we will never know.

I head for my sleeping bag at 8.30. For about half an hour I lie awake, listening to what seems to be aggressive chanting not far away. Is it another intimidating Sherpa rally taking place in the IMG camp? Is this the final straw, and where is the army to protect those who want to keep working? With the question unanswered I fall asleep.

DAY 22
SUMMIT MEETING

Thursday 24th of April, 2014 – Everest Base Camp, Nepal

I wake up long before breakfast and lie there pondering the events of the last day. Things have changed from hour to hour over the last week. This is normal for a mountaineering expedition, especially in the Himalayas, where the weather is fickle as a politician at election time. We get good weather forecasts on Everest these days, and they allow a fair degree of planning. But now it feels like the mood in camp is dictated by rumour – something much less predictable, and totally uncontrollable.

I have an acute feeling in the pit of my stomach that events are on a downward trajectory from which there is no return. My thoughts move from the machinations of militant Sherpas to the weakness of Nepal's government. The rally I believed I heard last night has reminded me how slow they are to act. Everest is the jewel in their tourist crown. Shouldn't they be more decisive than this?

A liaison officer said the demands would be met two days ago – or so we were told. There were also rumours about punishment for strikers. Yet still there has been no announcement, and the protests gather strength.

Often we hear about Sherpas threatening to break the legs of other Sherpas. If these rumours are true then the

Sherpas who want to keep working need urgent protection. Where is it? Nowhere to be seen. If there is an army presence here in Base Camp, as the government said there would be, then it must be somewhere in the clouds. Cloud cuckoo land, most likely.

I'm worried about Phil's meeting with the Ministry of Tourism. Were all the assurances he received nothing more than hot air?

I sit down to breakfast and learn that the rally I thought I heard last night was just the IMG team having a party. They are leaving, and wanted to enjoy their final evening here. That clears up one thing, at least. Is this how rumours start? I'm relieved to hear it, but it's one meaningless crumb of comfort.

Phil arrives on an eight o'clock helicopter just as we're starting breakfast. He cuts a forlorn figure as he walks alone from the helipad. A handful of us stand to welcome him. Edita gives him a hug and I pat him on the back. I feel very sorry for him. He is a good man doing his best, but everything seems to be unravelling.

More helicopters chug by overhead. We hurry over to the SPCC tent to be there when the delegation from the Ministry arrives. The grandstand mound is already full when I get there. I perch on a rock with Phil, Margaret and Caroline, affording us a good view of an area where chairs have been placed for the delegation to speak.

I ask Phil to point out Pasang Tenzing the troublemaker. I've heard so much about him from so many people, but I still don't know what he looks like. The man in the purple beanie looked to be the main ringleader at the puja.

It doesn't take Phil long to spot him. In fact, he could hardly have been more conspicuous. He sports a camouflage baseball cap with the logo 'L.A.' on it, and the truculent grin of a man puffed up with self-importance. He looks young, and reminds me of a Nepali Justin Bieber. I keep my eye on him throughout the events that follow, and measure the tide by his reaction.

The delegation arrives at 9.15 and promptly disappears into the SPCC tent. Pasang Tenzing slips in behind them. Most of them have flown here straight from Kathmandu, to an altitude which is dangerous for unacclimatised people. Oxygen sets are available should anyone need them. We know that there isn't much time before it's unsafe for them to remain here.

We are therefore puzzled when trays of Tibetan bread, tea and omelettes are taken into the tent. On this important occasion, when people's livelihoods are at stake, there is not a moment to lose for an agreement to be reached. But it seems that the first priority of the delegation from the Ministry is to take breakfast. We're at 5,300m. Couldn't they have eaten before they left Kathmandu?

After half an hour they emerge and take up their positions on the seats outside. Everyone crowds round to take photographs. I notice Pasang Tenzing take up a position crouched behind the Minister himself.

An earnest-looking man in a black jacket gets up to make a speech.[5] He looks honest and projects his voice so that everyone can hear what he is saying. Understanding him is another matter. He speaks in Nepali, and I have no idea what he is saying. After ten minutes he finishes, receiving polite applause from half the audience. Pasang remains crouching, unmoved. If the other half of the audience are expecting someone to translate it for us, we are disappointed.

Instead, a second man in an orange down jacket and topi hat gets up to speak. Again, he speaks only in Nepali.[6] Where the first speaker was sober, this man is impassioned, and angry about something. I see Pasang Tenzing stand up behind the Minister and gesticulate wildly to others in the crowd. Is this man in the jacket an official from the Ministry telling the agitators to go back to work? Whatever he is saying, Pasang isn't at all happy about it.

We never find out, because this speech isn't translated either.

A third man gets up and delivers a less impassioned speech.[7] He receives polite applause, but it doesn't matter what he says, because everyone is about to have their thunder stolen.

Ang Tshering Sherpa addresses the masses at the Base Camp summit meeting

The man in the purple beanie gets up and addresses the delegation.[8] Pasang appears to be cheerleading for him, spurring on the audience with frantic gestures. Sometimes the man in the purple hat elicits whoops of delight from some of the Sherpas in the grandstand. I have no idea what is being said, but I don't like it.

Just like the puja, it feels to me like this event has been taken over by the militants. This is not a meeting to reach an agreement and find a way forward, but another political rally. The protesters are in control and the delegation from the Ministry is doing nothing to stop them. Half the audience are westerners. We are the people who have paid tens of thousands to be here, and given these people work. Between us we put millions of dollars into the economy of Nepal.

If we had a voice, then we could contribute to this meeting. We support many of their demands. We want our millions of dollars to go to the victims' families, and we want better insurance in future years. There is a way forward if we all keep climbing.

But it's not only that we don't have a voice. We don't even have a pair of ears, because nobody has bothered to translate for us. It's as though we don't matter to them.

I no longer have the will to stand on a rock and listen to myself being shafted in Nepali. At 10.30, as I did at the puja, I step down from my perch and trudge back to camp, utterly dejected.

I lie in my tent and ponder. After half an hour I hear a rumble, followed by a loud cheer. When the others return to camp they tell me what happened. Everyone had moved over to the helipad to see the delegation off. As they were waiting, another chunk of ice broke off from exactly the same serac on the West Shoulder. The avalanche wasn't as big this time, but still it billowed across the Icefall in much the same way. It was late in the morning to be climbing through the ice, but had anyone been there it would have been serious.

In the old days this incident would have been laden with symbolism. It would be seen as a clear message from the mountain gods to keep away. They're not happy, and we shouldn't go into the Icefall.

But a loud cheer is very different from the awed silence you would expect from a deeply superstitious people reacting to a sign from the gods. These Sherpas are young and cynical. They don't believe in mountain gods any more than we do.

We all know what the avalanche means this time. It's all over. The protesters have won the battle. It's time for us to go home.

Is the Khumbu Icefall more dangerous this year? This is my first time here, so I don't know, but those seracs on the West Shoulder must have been there for many years. They will always have posed a risk. There are many ways it could be made safer, though. Firstly, the route could go more up the middle of the Icefall instead of passing underneath the Shoulder. Secondly, our Sherpas were complaining about the state of the ladders before the accident happened. It was a faulty ladder that led to so many Sherpas queuing in the worst possible place when the avalanche struck. Thirdly, fewer people in the Icefall at any one time would reduce the risk by allowing everyone to move more quickly. Finally, there are probably inexperienced Sherpas up there as well as inexperienced clients. Some of the Sherpas could do with better training, and some of the clients could do with better vetting. Put all these factors together and it's clear that the south side of Everest would definitely benefit from some much-needed regulation.

We sit crestfallen in the dining tent over tea. We feel like we've received a royal shafting, and there's little chance of any recompense. Phil reminds us that sixteen people died up there. It's their families we should be remembering. He is right, of course. I wish I could; it's what those men deserve. Edita lost her friend Dorje Khatri. Many of our Sherpas were close to the victims. How can we forget? In the last week my memory of that incident, the shocking sight of bodies airlifted by helicopter, has been swallowed up in a tidal wave of politics.

Phil has more reason than anyone to be bitter. He goes into the Sherpa tent to find out what was said at the gathering this morning, taking along the document that the officials from the Ministry gave him after their meeting. They told him this document was the copy of an agreement to meet the Sherpa demands. It was written in Nepali and he took their word for it. Our Sherpas tell him that it's not an agreement at all, but just a copy of the original Sherpa demands – the same ones that Trish pasted into an email days ago.

The officials from the Ministry said the demands would be met. They said an agreement would be given to the Sherpas. The Icefall Doctors would forge a new route through the Icefall, and strikers would be banned from working in future years. None of these things happened.

Today's event seems to have been a photocall for vain politicians and militant agitators. Perhaps things were discussed in the SPCC tent while they were eating omelettes and garlic soup, but it hardly seems likely, and any common ground was destroyed straight away. From what we saw there was no concerted effort to reach an agreement and find a way forward, no shred of an attempt to find a route out of a difficult situation to the satisfaction of everyone.

It's easy to sit there like those officials and do nothing, yet pretend that by being there you are doing something positive. In this sense I have a degree of respect for the protesters, much as I disagree with their actions. At least they did something, however misguided it was, and succeeded in their aims.

Dorje and Pasang Ongchu join us in the dining tent. I feel so sorry for them. They have worked like Trojans.

They have stood up to those in their community who sought to drive a wedge between us. They have remained loyal, honest and unbelievably cheerful. But to some people they will be tarred with the same brush as the militants, a brush that will be painted across the whole Sherpa community. It is likely they will all find it harder to get work next year.

Meanwhile Edita comes back from the meeting with a shocking story that sheds light on a possible reason why IMG cancelled their expedition without waiting for today's meeting. She spoke to one of their clients at the meeting. With great emotion they spoke of how one of their Sherpas had told them to leave within seven days, or they would break their legs.

One of their own Sherpas! If this proves to be true then it was nothing to do with protecting the Sherpas, but protecting the clients. At this stage it is still no more than a rumour; we don't know who the client is, or whether they were telling the truth. But in these circumstances it can't be easy for an operator, and they behaved appropriately. It would have left their leader with no choice. How could they stay on the mountain? It's doubtful even army personnel stationed at Base Camp could have resolved such differences.[9]

Not that the army were ever going to be stationed at Base Camp, any more than flying yaks would bring them here. I can't help thinking that the government is the real villain. They have taken our permit fees, liaison officer fees, and Icefall Doctor fees, and where did that money go? We were not permitted to climb; our liaison officer was nowhere to be seen; and now the Icefall Doctors are going home too. We won't get any of this money back, of course. We would love to climb with Dorje and Pasang Ongchu again, and help them to support their families. But to do so we have to pay more fees to the government first.

'The government all talk, no do,' Pasang says apologetically.

They won't blame us if we do not return, any more than we blame them for what's happened here. Will we climb together again after this expedition is over? I hope so, but I just don't know.

DAY 23
BEWILDERMENT

Friday 25th of April, 2014 – Everest Base Camp, Nepal

We had a long night drowning our sorrows and going through several boxes of wine that we no longer need. As usual, I feel hangover-free, but I'm in a state of shock about how this expedition has turned out. It's hard to believe it's all over, and we haven't even set foot above Base Camp.

Did I dream that farcical ceremony with the Ministry of Tourism that finally put us out of our misery?

The surreal situation is reinforced by the conditions this morning. There is a light dusting of snow on the ground, and the Base Camp amphitheatre is absolutely beautiful. How can such terrible things have happened here in the last week?

Over breakfast we agree to walk down to Pheriche tomorrow to catch helicopters back to Kathmandu. I am in no hurry to leave Nepal. My flight back to the UK is not until the end of May, and I vaguely remember having agreed, after a few glasses of wine last night, to trek up to the Annapurna Sanctuary with Margaret and Edita.

I spend the morning packing my things and preparing a blog post to send when I'm back in Kathmandu. Phil has agreed for two people from the Discovery Channel to come over to camp this morning and interview some of us about the season. They had intended to film a documentary about a man in a wingsuit flying off the summit, but they've ended up with a very different story to tell.

Several of the team agree to talk, but I prefer to steer clear. I'm still unsure of the story, and I don't want to go on camera to be misrepresented. In the end only Phil and Ricardo are interviewed.

Despite the depression in camp, we maintain our sense of humour. Phil tells his Sherpas that Trish is insisting they stay for another four weeks to complete the season and earn the rest of their pay.

Sangye ends this attempt at humour with a simple argument. 'I eat two meal of dal bhat a day. It cost 300 rupees a kilo to carry my shit down from Base Camp. We leave early, I save you money, boss.'

On a more sobering note, over dinner Phil talks for the first time in detail about what he saw at the avalanche site. Most of the victims died not from being buried alive, but from shards of ice exploding from the serac like shrapnel.

'There were decapitations up there,' he says.

I don't think I'm the only person at the table who feels sick. The event could have happened at any time. Had it been an hour later or an hour earlier, the outcome could have been different. Perhaps nobody would have died at all. But it happened at precisely the wrong moment and caused destruction in the most hideous way imaginable.

Nobody is in the mood for staying up late tonight and finishing the rest of Phil's wine. I leave the tent at 7.30 to head for bed. Only Jay and Ricardo remain there, arguing about religion. I still hear their voices murmuring a few metres away as I drift off to sleep.

DAY 24
ESCAPE FROM BASE CAMP

Saturday 26th of April, 2014 – Kathmandu, Nepal

The end is near. It's our earliest breakfast since we arrived at Base Camp, apart from that fateful day when we intended to climb into the Icefall. Our helicopters are booked to leave Pheriche at 2.30, and Phil says it will take three hours to walk there. Using the simple formula that any journey on foot takes twice as long as Phil says it will, I calculate that it will take us six hours to get there. We therefore need to leave early.

We take breakfast at seven o'clock. Afterwards I pack away my sleeping bag and all the other things I won't be needing for a while. Our kit bags have to be carried down by porters, and they won't arrive in Kathmandu until Wednesday. I'm the last to finish packing. I miss a group photo with our Sherpas, and my teammates have all left camp by the time I carry my kit bag to the storage tent. But Tarke, who is coming to Lukla with us to make sure everything is OK, is still waiting for me.

I soon catch up with the stragglers in the boulder fields on the fringes of camp. By the time I reach the moraine ridge I have overtaken them, and find myself walking alone for the next hour. It's an opportunity to contemplate our expedition and consider all the things that have happened in the last week and a day. Nothing seems to make sense.

I catch up with the remainder of the team – Robert, Jay, Kevin, Ian, Ricardo and Mel – a short distance beyond Gorak Shep. They are waiting for herds of yaks and trekkers coming the other way. Most of the trekkers look tired, but at least they won't be weighed down by the sense of dejection that we are. I wonder how many are even aware of the momentous events that have just taken place at their destination.

As for us, we move quickly, as though fleeing, which isn't far from the truth. I take consolation from the landscape. Whatever happens to humans here over the next few years, the scenery will remain peerless and majestic.

I stop for a rest and a drink at Lobuche, where our group divides. The speedsters – Kevin, Ian and Jay – disappear off in a puff of whatever it is that powers them. Ricardo and I leapfrog one another for the rest of the way. We stop for more photographs at the memorials above the Thok La. Ama Dablam forms a pinnacled backdrop, and I wonder how long it will be before there are sixteen more cairns here.

We need to check Ricardo's map to find the trail down to Pheriche, as we took a different route on the way up. An obvious trail leads down a gully to a broad valley. We are now some distance beneath the high plateau we crossed after leaving Dingboche seventeen days ago. I see Pheriche in the distance ahead, but Ricardo is even more anxious than me to reach it. He overtakes me at a run; I don't bother trying to keep up.

I cross streams and yak pastures, and reach the village some way behind him. I walk into a likely looking teahouse that advertises free Wi-Fi. There's nobody there that I know, but a little further along Jay emerges from another one wearing his cowboy hat. They have chosen this particular teahouse because it is right next to the helipad. Ian, Kevin, Ricardo and Mel are sitting inside drinking San Miguel beer.

Memorial cairns at the Thok La, with Kangtega rising up behind

It's barely 11.30, and for once Phil was right about the time. We have raced down here, keen to get away from this dream world of high mountains that offered so much, but left us disappointed, sad and bewildered.

It toys with us one last time. By 2.30 a grey mist has enveloped the valley and there is little chance of a helicopter landing. It seems that there is nothing we can do but drink more beer and accept that we must spend the night in Pheriche. But at four o'clock, when the mist seems as thick as ever and there is still no hope of getting out of here tonight, we hear the sound of helicopter blades somewhere overhead.

We couldn't have reacted more quickly had a yak charged into the teahouse, aimed its horns at our table, and started pawing the ground. We leave our beers unfinished and rush outside with our packs.

Two helicopters have landed on the scrubby field behind the teahouse. How many of us will be able to pile in? I'd heard that at this altitude they will only fly with a maximum of four passengers. More in hope than expectation, I try to squeeze in as a fifth passenger, resting my pack on my knees. The pilot doesn't try to stop me. I'm even more surprised when Tarke gestures for me to move up, and he jumps in beside.

The doors are closed and we feel the chopper rising off the ground. Everything seems to happen so fast. The cloud has evaporated, and within an instant we are flying down a forested valley, with Tengboche Monastery on a ridge below us.

There is a repeat performance after we land at the helipad in Lukla a few minutes later. It's only 4.30, and here in the Dudh Khosi Valley, 2,000m lower down, it's a beautiful afternoon. The rest of our team managed to squeeze on to the second chopper, and we are all here. It seems like there's a good chance we'll be back in Kathmandu tonight after all.

But there are only two choppers, and another team is already boarding one of them. A representative of the helicopter company approaches me.

'Only six on first helicopter,' he says.

'But it will fly to Kathmandu and come back for the others tonight?' I ask him.

'Maybe,' he says, but he doesn't look hopeful.

'Women and children first,' I hear someone say.

That means Margaret, Edita and Caroline. We give Mel a seat because his wife is arriving in Kathmandu tonight. I'm a little surprised, and more than a little pleased, when

Ian and I are given the other two seats. I can only assume this is because they regard us as children.

I can hardly believe my luck. I don't think any of us can. Within seconds we are inside again. The chopper rises from the ground and we are flying over forested ridges and miles of rice terraces. We are all grinning like children now. Edita sits in the passenger seat in front of me. She turns her head, and her smile is as wide as the South Col.

What an expedition. Was it a holiday or an ordeal? A dream or a nightmare? I think it will be a long time before we know.

EXPEDITION DISPATCH
THE DOUBLE EVEREST TRAGEDY

Footsteps on the Mountain Blog – Sunday 27th of April, 2014

I'm back in Kathmandu again at the end of what has effectively been a very expensive Everest Base Camp trek. All expeditions have now been cancelled, and there will not be a single summit from Everest's south side this season.

This has been without a doubt one of the most bizarre experiences of my life, and I'm still in a state of shock trying to make sense of it all. I wanted to climb Lhotse this year because I climbed Everest from the north side two years ago, and I wanted to sample the south-side experience without having to climb the mountain for a second time. Lhotse shares its route with Everest for much of the way up. Where Everest climbers continue across the Lhotse Face to the South Col which divides the two mountains, we were intending to divert up the face to Lhotse's summit.

I wanted to sleep in the grand amphitheatre of Everest Base Camp, surrounded by impossibly precipitous peaks – Pumori, Lingtren, Khumbutse, Nuptse and Everest's West Shoulder, which appears as an imposing peak in its own right from there. I wanted to climb through the ice towers and seracs of the Khumbu Icefall, and stand in the Western

Cwm, named by George Mallory after the hills of Snowdonia and christened the Valley of Silence by the Swiss team who first stood there in 1952. I wanted to climb up the Lhotse Face and look across the South Col to Everest. These are places I have read so much about, and I would love to have seen them for myself, but it didn't happen.

But I also wanted to sample the south-side Everest experience because it receives so much negative attention in the media, and I wanted to find out for myself whether it's as much of a circus as people make out. I found the answer to that. Boy, did I find the answer. Never in my wildest nightmares did I imagine it would be like this. One thing I didn't expect was a circus built by Nepalis rather than western climbers.

I am posting this having not read a single sentence of what has been written in the media about this year's Everest season. I will read all that soon enough I'm sure, but for now these are my thoughts alone. My phone has been switched off, and only once did I wander down to Gorak Shep to send a blog post and check messages. I have been scribbling furiously in my diary about the events I have witnessed, but at times it's been difficult to find the words. It's certainly too early to make sense of it all. I have plenty to say, but for now I will keep it brief.

A small number of militant agitators have chosen to exploit a terrible tragedy to pursue their own agenda, and a corrupt and ineffectual government has stood by and watched. This has magnified the tragedy and made it more likely those Sherpas caught in the avalanche of 18 April died in vain. It has also ensured we are all losers here: Sherpas, government, western climbers and mountaineering operators.

I expect a lot of people are coming in for criticism at the moment, so I would just like to stick up for a few people.

Since the very hour of the tragedy our own thirty-strong Sherpa team from Altitude Junkies have been solid as a rock. They have stood squarely beside us, remained friendly, loyal and cheerful, stayed out of the politics and waited patiently for the opportunity to climb. They are honest, humble folk who are here to support their families and continue the rich tradition of Himalayan mountaineering that has made the Sherpas prosperous and world famous. We know many of them from previous expeditions and they remain our friends. Our sirdar Dorje Sherpa is a legend in the Khumbu region, and a hero in the eyes of us all in the Altitude Junkies team. Wizened and wise, we all look up to him, Sherpas and westerners alike. If only there were more like him the militants would never have been able to get their way. It's likely Everest will be quiet next season, but all our guys deserve to find work.

Our expedition leader Phil Crampton is also an unsung hero. He has invested a great deal in Nepal over the years and taken great financial risk. He does not make millions out of mountaineering here. It's no coincidence that eight of our team are repeat Junkies clients. We know he runs one of the best expeditions on the mountain, but also one of the cheapest. Events have proven that he also has the most loyal Sherpas.

Phil flew to Kathmandu at his own expense last week to negotiate with the government and try to save the season. They let him down. He was promised much, but given nothing. Like all operators he has hundreds of kilos of equipment stuck up in the Western Cwm. Yesterday eight teams each sent a Sherpa up there by helicopter to gather it together. It will stay up there, frozen in and moving with the glacier. Perhaps it will be retrievable next year, if any of them decide to come back here.

But Phil doesn't seem to be worrying about his own losses. He worries about his Sherpas, some of whom may not be able find work if he has to pull out of Nepal. And he worries about us – his clients, who have paid him a great deal of money and haven't even left Base Camp. We feel like we've been stitched up, but not by him.

It started as a terrible, random tragedy, with no blame and no villains, but it has become something else. From what I have seen westerners have behaved appropriately. I don't know what has been said to the media, but around camp we have been silent, patient and sensitive. These are people, many of whom have saved up and trained for years to be here, mortgaged their houses, quit jobs, made career and relationship sacrifices, all for nothing. A few operators who have accepted their money and employed militants have actions to take in the coming months.

I believe the biggest share of the responsibility lies with the government. The militants are mostly kids who haven't considered the consequences of their actions. They will harm themselves and their community in the long run. The government talk endlessly about what they intend to do here, and end up doing nothing. Long before the season began they promised police and army at Base Camp to avoid a repeat of the fight that occurred here last year. Had that happened the intimidation that has prevented people climbing could have been avoided. To great fanfare they announced we would each have to carry eight kilograms of trash down from the higher camps, but now there are several tons of additional equipment lying on Chomolungma's slopes.

I'm going to stop ranting now. It's still too early and emotions are raw. The last week has felt like a year. So much has happened that it's easy for me to forget that I watched sixteen people lose their lives in a hideous, unparalleled tragedy that but for a few hours, or a few more metres of climbing, might have taken me as well.

Wasn't that enough?

EPILOGUE
ONE YEAR ON

Saturday 25ᵗʰ of April, 2015 – London, United Kingdom

When I looked up that day and saw the giant cloud of snow billowing across the Khumbu Icefall, and watched the helicopter bring body after body down on longlines, I never thought I would ever think of it as a straightforward climbing accident.

Everest has seen its share of multiple tragedies. As early as 7 June 1922, seven of George Mallory's Sherpas lost their lives in an avalanche on the North Col Wall. More famously, eight climbers died in a storm on 11 May 1996, an event described by Jon Krakauer in his book *Into Thin Air*. Six people died in separate incidents on the day I reached the summit myself, the 19 May 2012.

The avalanche I witnessed on the 18 April 2014 trumped them all by some margin. Sixteen Sherpas lost their lives, and I found myself caught up in events beyond my ability to comprehend. I had seen strikes by mountain workers before. In Pakistan in 2009 our progress up the Baltoro Glacier was halted when our porters woke up to snow and decided to stay put that day. In Nepal the following year some of our porters refused to move one morning during the trek to Baruntse. Our sirdar, the same Dawa I met at Everest Base Camp during the puja-cum-rally, resolved it by reweighing their loads.

The events of 2014 were quite different, and unprecedented. Protests were more organised; there were leaders and speeches. Demands were issued. There was an undercurrent of violence.

I returned to Kathmandu shocked and bewildered. The avalanche had been traumatic, but it was easy to make sense of. The events that followed made my brain hurt. It was obvious there was something going on I didn't understand.

As I'd expected, a media storm followed. It was almost entirely negative. We had seen a complex series of events, but the media focus was to blame western climbers and operators for what happened. Journalists often contacted me when I returned to Kathmandu, but I didn't want to talk. I was still trying to make sense of things, and I didn't want anyone putting words into my mouth. I could do that myself on my blog.

But I knew one thing for certain: I had no wish to return to Lhotse. I had learned what I needed about the south-side Everest experience, and I didn't like it. It seemed quite probable to me that something unpleasant would happen again.

That was just my opinion, though. Many people who had their dreams shattered in 2014 decided to return the following year.

One of these was Edita. We had started dating when we returned to Kathmandu, and we discussed Everest a lot over the following months. She was not as cynical as me, and still harboured a desire to return. Margaret also chose to go back in 2015. And, of course, Phil and our old Sherpa friends Dorje, Pasang Ongchu, Chongba and Tarke were there as usual.

I was right about there being something unpleasant, but it happened in a way I could never have imagined.

Things were going well. A safer, steeper route had been found up the middle of the Khumbu Icefall. Edita and Margaret had just been up into the ice for a few hours.

When I woke up at home in London on Saturday, 25 April, the first thing I did was check my email. Edita had sent me a blog post to publish about her first climb into the Icefall.

I never got around to posting it for her, because a few minutes later a news item caught my eye.

The Junkies were taking it easy back in Base Camp that morning. Edita was drinking tea in the dining tent with Phil. As they sat talking they noticed the table starting to rattle, gradually at first, then faster and faster. They knew it was an earthquake, but there was nothing they could do. It continued for ninety seconds, but it seemed much longer.

When the shaking stopped they ran outside. They were OK, but what about the rest of the team?

They had no time to find out. Phil's eyes were bulging like bowling balls as he looked up the hillside above camp. Edita followed his gaze and to her horror she saw something that brought the previous year's avalanche into sharp focus, before shattering it like exploding glass. High overhead Pumori was collapsing in a giant cloud of snow and rock. It dwarfed the avalanche we had seen in the Khumbu Icefall and it was heading straight towards them.

'Get back in the tent, get back in the tent,' Phil screamed.

Shrieks of terror were echoing around camp. They raced back into the dining tent and fell down on the ground. A split second later they felt the impact as tons of debris pounded the roof above them. It lasted for another minute, but the tent held firm.

They had escaped death by the length of an ice axe. In less than five minutes Base Camp had been turned into a war zone. The whole of the central part of camp looked like it had been shelled. The Junkies' storage tents were totally destroyed, but their sleeping tents and the dining tent were just outside the danger zone. Everyone in the team had survived without serious injury. It was a miracle.

But their ordeal was only just beginning. Edita could see injured people walking like wounded soldiers. Some were being carried towards IMG's camp to receive help. It was only then that she realised the whole middle part of Base Camp had been wiped out.

They spent the rest of the day helping the injured. They carried boxes of medical supplies and injured climbers to camps that had been set up for triage and treatment. Many people were injured or dead. The previous year we had been sheltered from the full horror, but this time there was no way to avoid it. At the end of the day they returned to the Junkies' camp and sat silently in the dining tent. There was blood on the table cloth, but it was not their own. They were completely shell-shocked, and nobody could speak a word.

The work wasn't finished, and the following day they had to recover bodies from the wreckage of camp. Edita helped Phil to dig up one of the dead, and what she saw was too horrible to describe. A tent had been thrown hundreds of metres over a cliff. The body was all broken, and so much of it was missing that it no longer looked human. They knew how easily it could have been one of them, but by a random twist of fate it was not.

Unlike the previous year, when for a week we still hoped to continue our expedition, this time they knew it was out of the question. The earthquake had destroyed the route through the Khumbu Icefall, leaving hundreds of climbers stranded at Camps 1 and 2 in the Western Cwm. Regular aftershocks wrecked more of the route, and brought avalanches tumbling down from both sides. The stranded climbers eventually had to leave by helicopter in a series of evacuations that had been well rehearsed the previous year.

The Junkies couldn't evacuate from camp, because the helicopters were for rescue only. The following days were calmer, but for Edita they were terrifying. She couldn't sleep, because aftershocks continued to rock camp. Avalanches roared down every few minutes, and while Base Camp is usually a place of security, this time nobody could be sure. She moved in with Margaret, and every time an avalanche fell, they sat up and held each other. It was stressful for everyone, clients and Sherpas alike. They were all traumatised, and lived in fear of the next tremor.

They didn't know what was happening in the rest of Nepal, but after a few days I was able to send text messages. I told Edita what I had learned from news reports. My own experience of the earthquake was trivial compared with theirs, but it wasn't pleasant either.

When I learned that there had been a 7.8-magnitude earthquake close to Kathmandu, my immediate thought was not that buildings were demolished, and thousands must be dead in Nepal's capital – instead I realised that such a powerful earthquake must have triggered another serac collapse on the West Shoulder. There was a high chance of more casualties in the Khumbu Icefall.

I believed that Edita was not among them because I knew she was back at Everest Base Camp. I sent her a text message to see if everyone was OK, but then I glanced through my Twitter timeline.

Twitter is not a nice place during an emergency. There were lots of rumours, and some of what I read caused me to shudder.

@alexgaven: Everest base camp huge earthquake then huge avalanche from pumori. Running for life from my tent. Unhurt.

Many many people up the mountain.

@ivanbraun: MIDCAMP ON SOUTH SIDE WIPED OUT, MANY PEOPLE MISSING.

@alexgaven: Huge disaster. Helped search and rescue victims through huge debris area. Many dead. Much more badly injured. More to die if not heli asap.

For the next four hours I didn't know whether Edita, or my other friends at Base Camp, were dead or alive. She usually responded to my messages almost immediately, but this time I heard nothing. I scoured every source I could for information. I wandered around the park opposite my home in a daze. After what seemed an eternity I received news from a mutual friend on Facebook. She told me that all of the Altitude Junkies team were alive, if not entirely safe. Margaret had managed to call her husband by satellite phone.

The earthquake had triggered another huge ice collapse on the ridge between Pumori and Lingtren. This time, climbers in the Icefall turned out to be in the safest possible place, although they found themselves stranded as the route fell away beneath them. The collapse sent an avalanche powering through the middle of Base Camp, boulders flying like missiles. Nineteen people were killed, but the tents on either edge of camp were spared.

What happened in 2014 troubled me greatly for several months afterwards, but it was simpler than I thought. Essentially we had watched a climbing accident, followed by a labour dispute. We waited in expectation for a week, then went home dejected. For sixteen families life would never be the same, but for everyone else it continued much as it ever had.

The events of 2014 were quite minor compared to the 2015 earthquake. Outside Base Camp in 2015 more than

8,000 people were dead and thousands more were homeless. For two or three days parts of Kathmandu were without power or water, and people slept outside for fear of another major quake. It was some time before news filtered in from remoter parts of Nepal. Over a hundred trekkers were missing in the Langtang region, and Langtang village was completely destroyed.

Many teams at Base Camp didn't know about the situation outside. They feared that hotels would be closed in Kathmandu and teahouses destroyed on the Everest Base Camp trail. Some chose to brave the unknown dangers of Base Camp and wait for news rather than trek to Lukla for a flight to Kathmandu. The Junkies team elected to stay, and when they left it was with a great deal of relief.

The media turned their attention to Nepal again, but this time the situation was different. There was sensational reporting, but not the tabloid-style blame of the previous year. In 2015 many more film crews and journalists travelled to Base Camp hoping for a story, but Everest reporting had improved since 2014. Journalists had done more homework.

They got their story, but it wasn't one they expected. This time it was a clear tale of natural disaster without blame. While there were stories of human error and conflict too, they were outweighed by the positive human stories.

Hope didn't last. Aid poured into Nepal, but as I write these words, much of it remains unspent. Nepal's politics remain impenetrable and insoluble.

Meanwhile Everest is still majestic. It towers aloof and unconcerned by the human intrigue that continues at its feet.

Edita lights a butter lamp for her friend Dorje Khatri and the other victims of the 2014 Everest avalanche

ACKNOWLEDGEMENTS

Thanks to the other members of my Everest and Lhotse team, including Caroline, Ian, Jay, Louis, Kevin, Margaret, Mel, Peter, Ricardo and Robert, for their patience and company.

I will never forget our amazing Sherpa crew for their cheerfulness, kindness and dignity in trying circumstances. My heartfelt thanks to all of them, including Ang Gelu, Chongba, Da Pasang, Kami Neru, Pasang Ongchu, and Tarke.

I reserve my deepest gratitude for Dorje, a hero and a gentleman.

To Phil Crampton for bearing the stress without losing his head.

To Edita Nichols for her moving account of the Nepal earthquake, and for being the silver lining.

To my editor, Alex Roddie, for his help polishing the text.

To all of you, readers of my blog and diaries. I hope you have enjoyed this one, and I look forward to welcoming you back sometime.

DEDICATION

This book is dedicated to the sixteen who lost their lives on 18 April 2014:

Mingma Nuru Sherpa
Dorji Sherpa
Ang Tshiri Sherpa
Tenzing Chottar Sherpa
Nima Sherpa
Phurba Ongyal Sherpa
Lakpa Tenjing Sherpa
Chiring Ongchu Sherpa
Dorje Khatri
Then Dorje Sherpa
Phur Temba Sherpa
Pasang Karma Sherpa
Asman Tamang
Angkaji Sherpa
Ash Bahadur Gurung
Pemba Tenji Sherpa

NOTES

1. The Discovery Channel released a one-hour documentary of the tragedy not long afterwards. It appeared on YouTube while I was still in Kathmandu, and I watched it in the courtyard of our hotel. I appeared for about three seconds, right at the start of the film. 'A huge avalanche swept across the entire width of the Icefall,' I croaked in an oxygen-depleted voice.

2. We find out later that the government offered derisory compensation of 40,000 Nepalese Rupees (around $400 USD) to each of the victims' families.

3. Two years later I went to the cinema to see a documentary film about the tragedy, *Sherpa – Trouble on Everest*, and was surprised to see Dawa appear briefly, addressing a gathering at Base Camp.

4. I learn later that this is Pasang Bhote, who was working for one of the Nepali agencies. Our UIAGM-qualified guide Pasang Ongchu, who knows most people in the Nepali climbing scene, told me that he had never seen this man at an expedition base camp before. Nor did he know whom he was working for.

5. Pasang Sherpa, a representative of the Nepal National Mountain Guide Association (NNMGA), not to be confused with Pasang Tenzing Sherpa, or

our own Pasang Ongchu Sherpa.

6. Ramesh Dhamala, President of the Trekking Agencies' Association of Nepal (TAAN).

7. Ang Tshering Sherpa, President of the Nepal Mountaineering Association (NMA).

8. Pasang Bhote, whose status was unclear, but who appeared to be the leader of the protesters.

9. Although another argument I heard much later from people who worked closely with Sherpas, was that Sherpas often threaten to break each other's legs without really meaning it, and that it was not a threat that should be taken literally. As Simone Moro discovered, some words sound worse in a different language.

SEVEN STEPS FROM SNOWDON TO EVEREST

A hill walker's journey to the top of the world

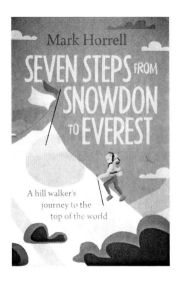

As he teetered on a narrow rock ledge a yak's bellow short of the stratosphere, with a rubber mask strapped to his face, a pair of mittens the size of a sealion's flippers, and a drop of two kilometres below him, it's fair to say Mark Horrell wasn't entirely happy with the situation he found himself in.

He was an ordinary hiker who had only read books about mountaineering, and little did he know when he signed up for an organised trek in Nepal with a group of elderly ladies that ten years later he would be attempting to climb the world's highest mountain.

But as he travelled across the Himalayas, Andes, Alps and East Africa, following in the footsteps of the pioneers, he dreamed up a seven-point plan to gain the skills and experience which could turn a wild idea into reality.

Funny, incisive and heartfelt, his journey provides a refreshingly honest portrait of the joys and torments of a modern-day Everest climber.

First published in 2015. A list of bookstores can be found on Mark's website:

www.markhorrell.com/SnowdonToEverest

PHOTOGRAPHS

I hope you enjoyed the photos in this book. Thanks to the miracles of the internet you can view all the photos from my Lhotse expedition online via the photo-sharing website *Flickr*.

Everest Base Camp. Nepal, April 2014:
www.markhorrell.com/EverestBaseCamp

ABOUT THE AUTHOR

For five years Mark Horrell has written what has been described as one of the most credible Everest opinion blogs out there. He writes about trekking and mountaineering from the often silent perspective of the commercial client.

For over a decade he has been exploring the world's greater mountain ranges and keeping a diary of his travels. As a writer he strives to do for mountain history what Bill Bryson did for long-distance hiking.

Several of his expedition diaries are available as quick reads from the major online bookstores. His first full-length book, *Seven Steps from Snowdon to Everest*, about his ten-year journey from hill walker to Everest climber, was published in November 2015.

His favourite mountaineering book is *The Ascent of Rum Doodle* by W.E. Bowman.

ABOUT THIS SERIES

The *Footsteps on the Mountain Travel Diaries* are Mark's expedition journals. Quick reads, they are lightly edited versions of what he scribbles in his tent each evening after a day in the mountains.

For other titles in this series see Mark's website:
www.markhorrell.com/diaries

CONNECT

You can join Mark's **mailing list** to keep updated:
www.markhorrell.com/mailinglist

Website and blog: www.markhorrell.com
Twitter: @markhorrell
Facebook:
www.facebook.com/footstepsonthemountain
Flickr: www.flickr.com/markhorrell
YouTube: www.youtube.com/markhorrell

DID YOU ENJOY THIS BOOK?

Thank you for buying and reading this book. Word-of-mouth is crucial for any author to be successful. If you enjoyed it then please consider leaving a review. Even if it's only a couple of sentences, it would be a great help and will be appreciated enormously.

Links to this book on the main online book stores can be found on Mark's website:

www.markhorrell.com/TheEverestPoliticsShow

CPSIA information can be obtained
at www.ICGtesting.com
Printed in the USA
LVOW11s0759120418
573235LV00001B/172/P